UNIFORMS OF THE THIRD REICH

UNIFORMS OF THE THIRD REICH

A Study in Photographs

Arthur Hayes & Jon Maguire

Schiffer Military History
Atglen, PA

Book Design by Robert Biondi

Library of Congress Control Number: 97-67432

ISBN: 978-0-7643-0358-6
Printed in China

Published by Schiffer Publishing, Ltd.
4880 Lower Valley Road
Atglen, PA 19310
Phone: (610) 593-1777; Fax: (610) 593-2002
E-mail: Info@schifferbooks.com
Web: www.schifferbooks.com

Introduction

German uniforms of World War II are among the most beautiful of any country's throughout history. The quality and craftsmanship of tailoring and manufacturing was extremely high, especially in the early years of the Reich.

The world of collecting German militaria of World War II grows a little more cloudy each year due to unscrupulous individuals who continue to perpetrate fraud on the unsuspecting collector by manufacturing fake items of all descriptions. As a result, collectors and historians alike are clamoring for more detailed information and access to genuine items of the period for study and comparison. This book takes a close look at a variety of authentic German uniforms of World War II including examples from the Army, Luftwaffe, Kriegsmarine, Waffen-SS, Allgemeine-SS, Hitler Youth and Political Leaders. The pieces are photographed in painstaking detail to show the reader tailor's tags, buttons, insignia detail, etc., and allow the reader to see what the genuine article looks like. Various accoutrements worn with the uniforms are also included to aid the reader. The authors hope that these photographs will broaden knowledge and help avoid the expensive pitfalls we have all had to deal with over the years.

We have made our best effort to insure that all items pictured are 100% genuine and we believe them to be so, but we do not claim to be infallible. If any items not of the World War II era have slipped passed us, we sincerely apologize.

While recognizing the Germans of World War II as a magnificent fighting force, this work is not intended to glorify them or their twisted political views. It is simply a photographic record of some of the clothing they wore. We must never forget!

Thanks to Susan Hayes, Rhonda Maguire, Pat Moran, Matthew Reinert (Military History Shop), Bill Shea, Bill Dienna, Mike Conner, The Hobby Shop, Mike Davidson, The Hussar, Bob Biondi and Peter Schiffer for their assistance on this project.

1

Army

The Parade Dress Uniform of an NCO of the Infantry "Regiment Grossdeutschland"

This uniform was introduced in March of 1939 to be worn from September 15, 1939. The tunic has two notable and distinct features. The collar patches and the cuff patterns are of a design completely different from all other German Army uniforms, to identify this elite unit with the traditions of the old Imperial Army. The uniform is shown here by itself and with the standard bearer 's carrying sash.

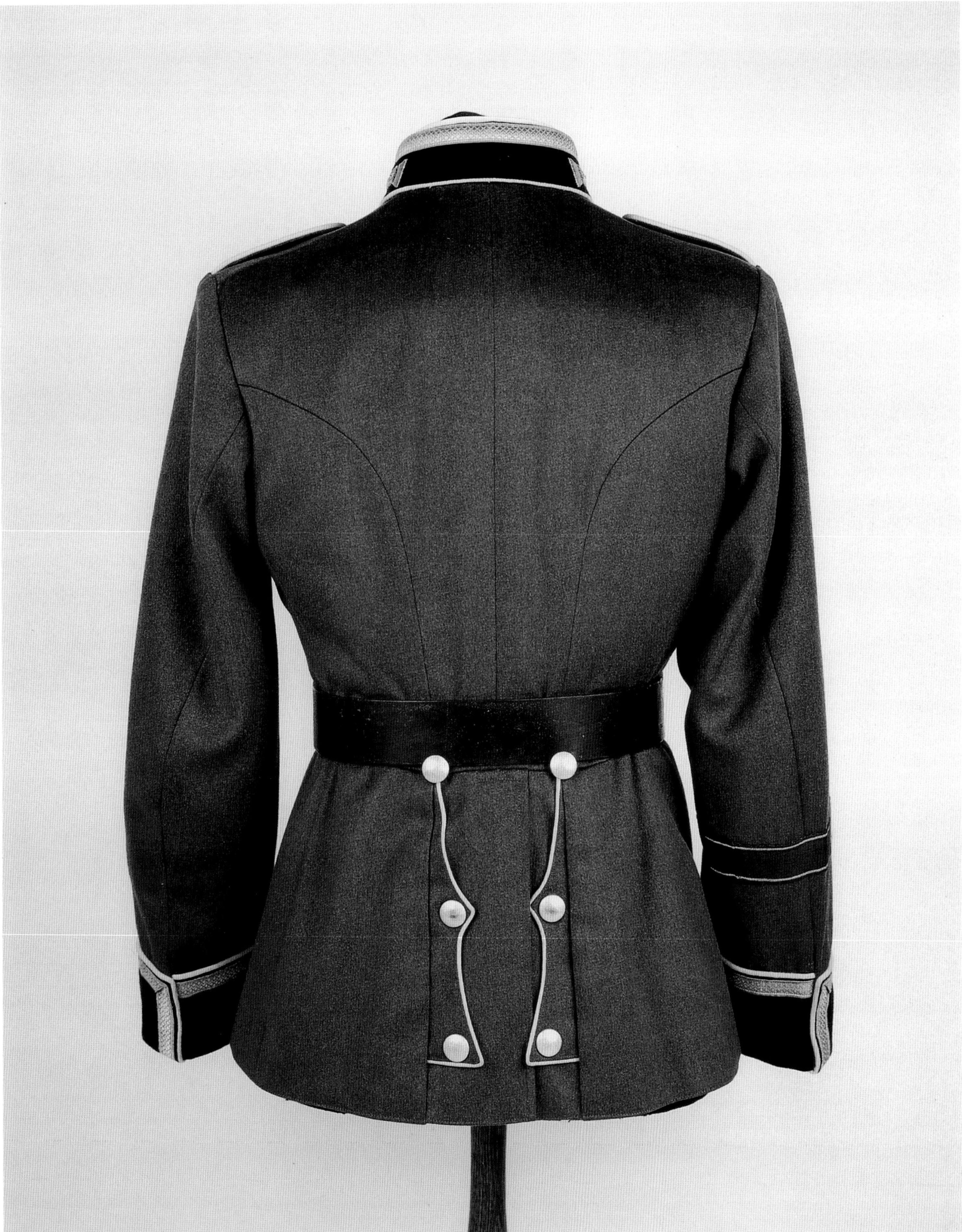

Großdeutschland

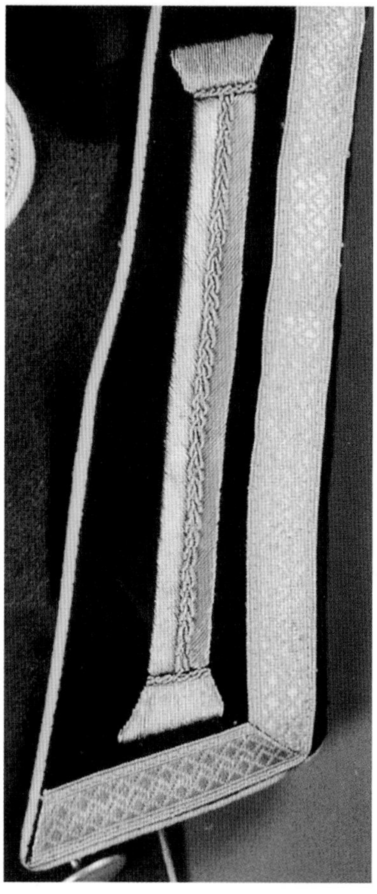

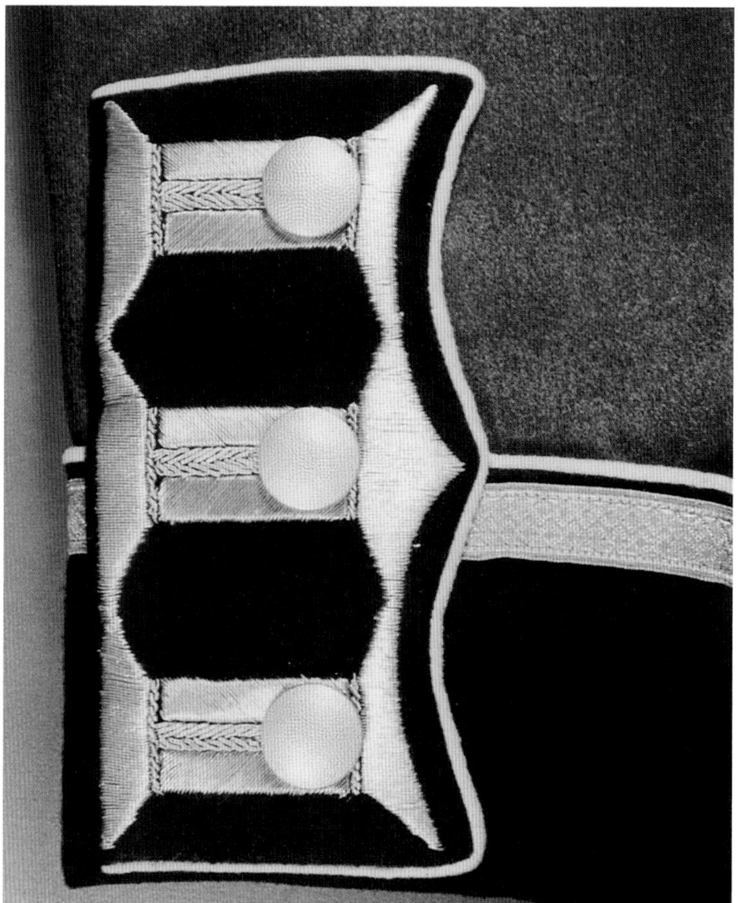

Großdeutschland

CIVIL UND UNIFORMEN
Melchior
KASSEL

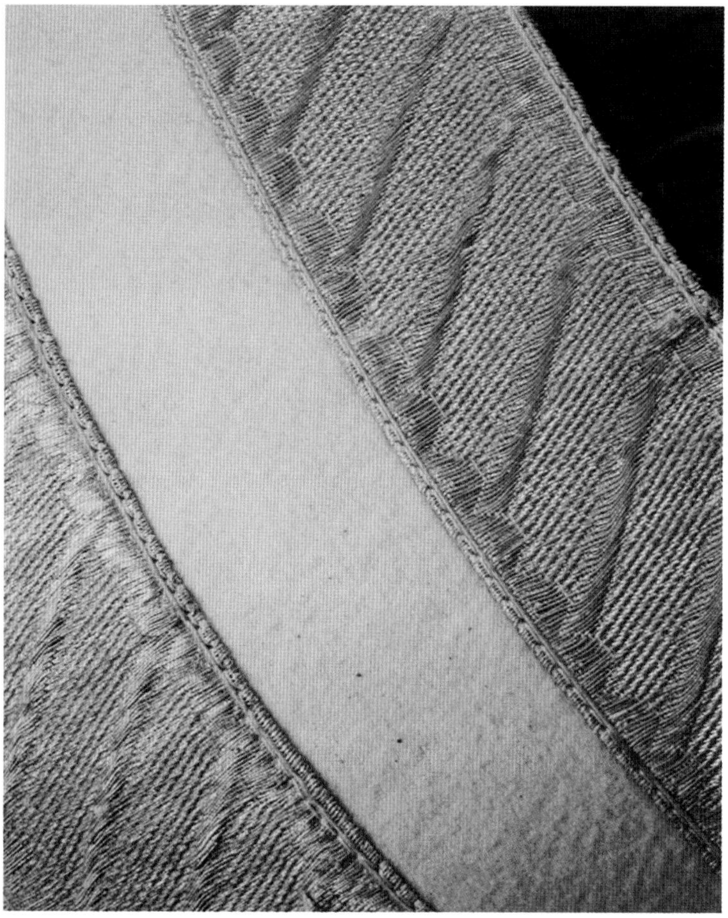

Detail of the bullion work on the standard bearer's sash.

Maker's mark on standard bearer's sash.

Infantry NCO's dress visor cap.

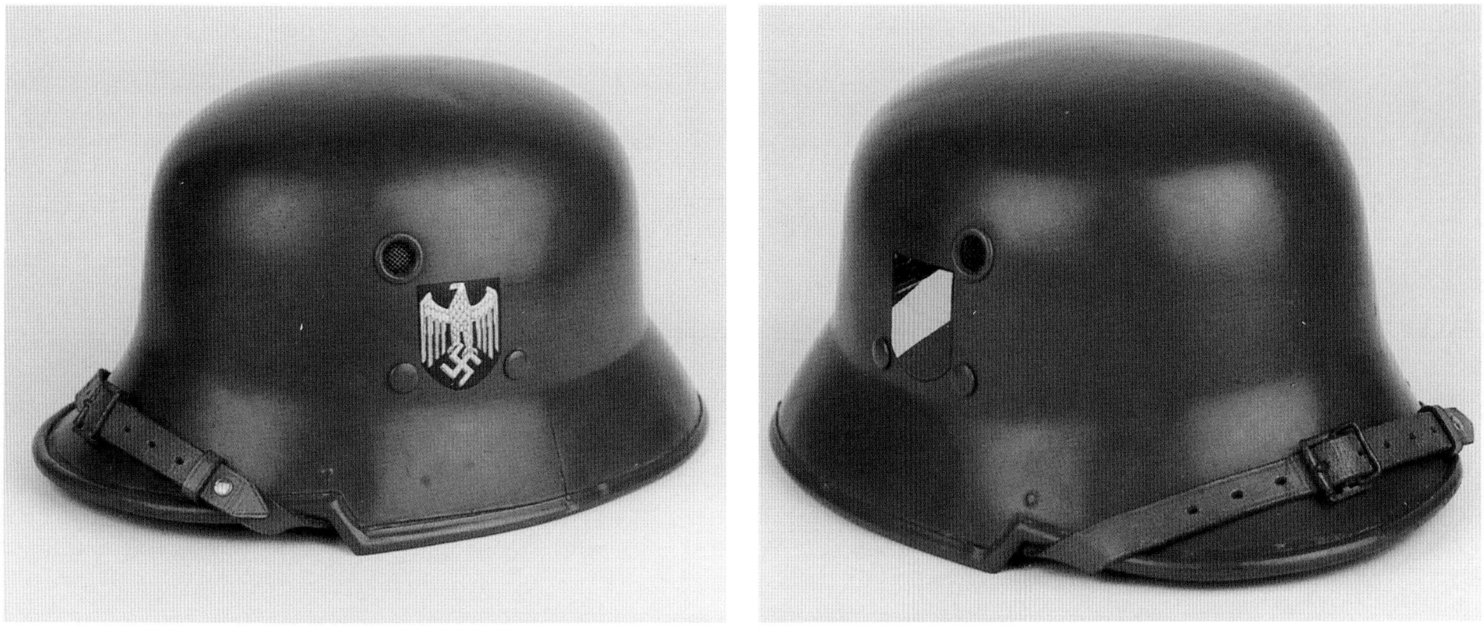

Parade dress vulcan fiber double decal helmet made by EREL.

EREL maker's mark on leather liner of fiber helmet.

Three examples of the "Grossdeutschland" cuff title.

Großdeutschland

The Army standard bearer's gorget. Right: Detail of chain links on gorget.

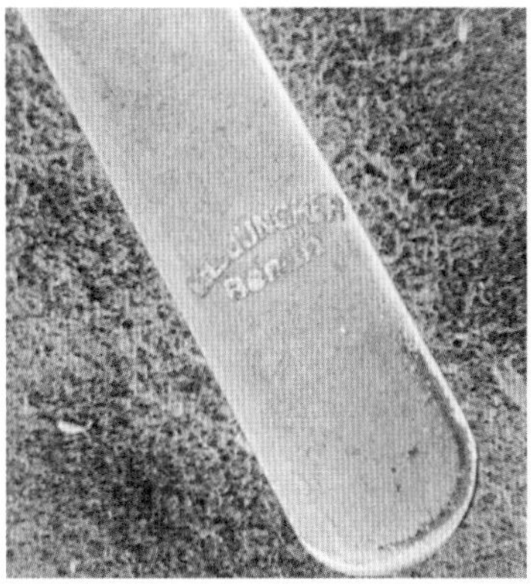

Left: C.E. Juncker hallmark on gorget. Right: Detail of maker's marking. Note solder where the base of the swastika joins the frame.

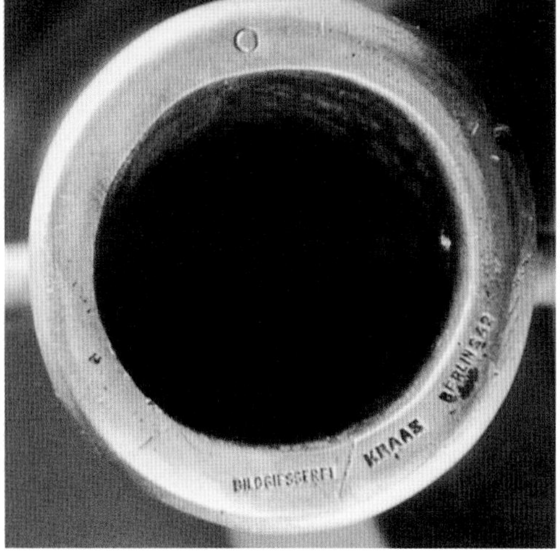

Hallmarks on pole top.

Army standard pole top device.

Uniform of Generalleutnant Hans von Kempski

This style of uniform was introduced in June of 1935. This example, dated 10-1-40, is named to Generalleutnant Hans von Kempski, who was the commander of the 199th Infantry Division. He was born 6-2-1883. The unusual white cloth Maltese Cross on the pocket is the Order of St. John of Jerusalem "Johanniter Order."

1939

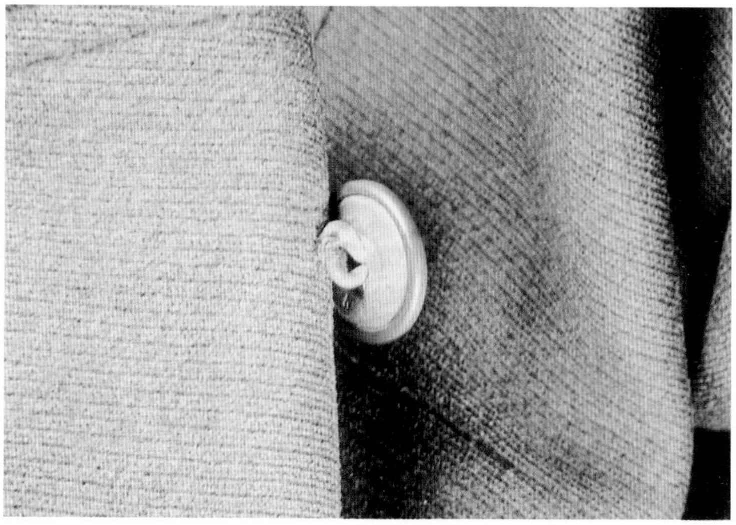

Blitz
KLEIN-UMSTADT

Generalleutnant von Kempski.

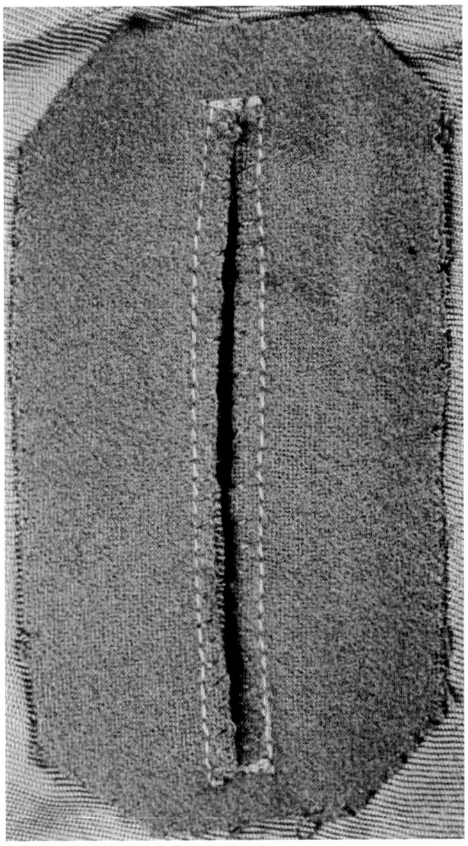

Detail of the opening inside the tunic for the dagger hangers to pass through.

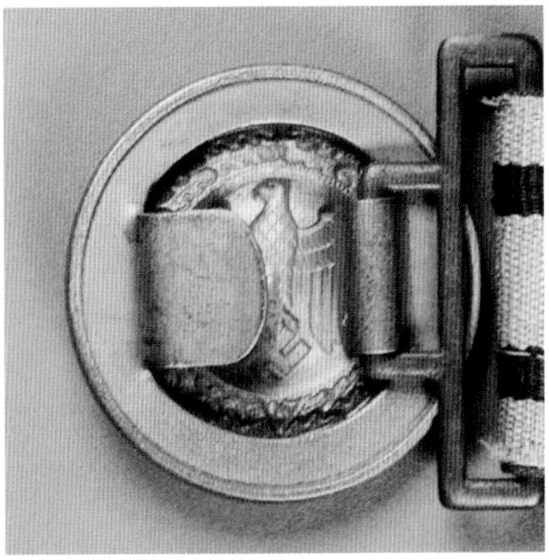

Two at right: Detail of the General Officer's Parade Dress belt and buckle.

Army General Officer's Great Coat dated 1936

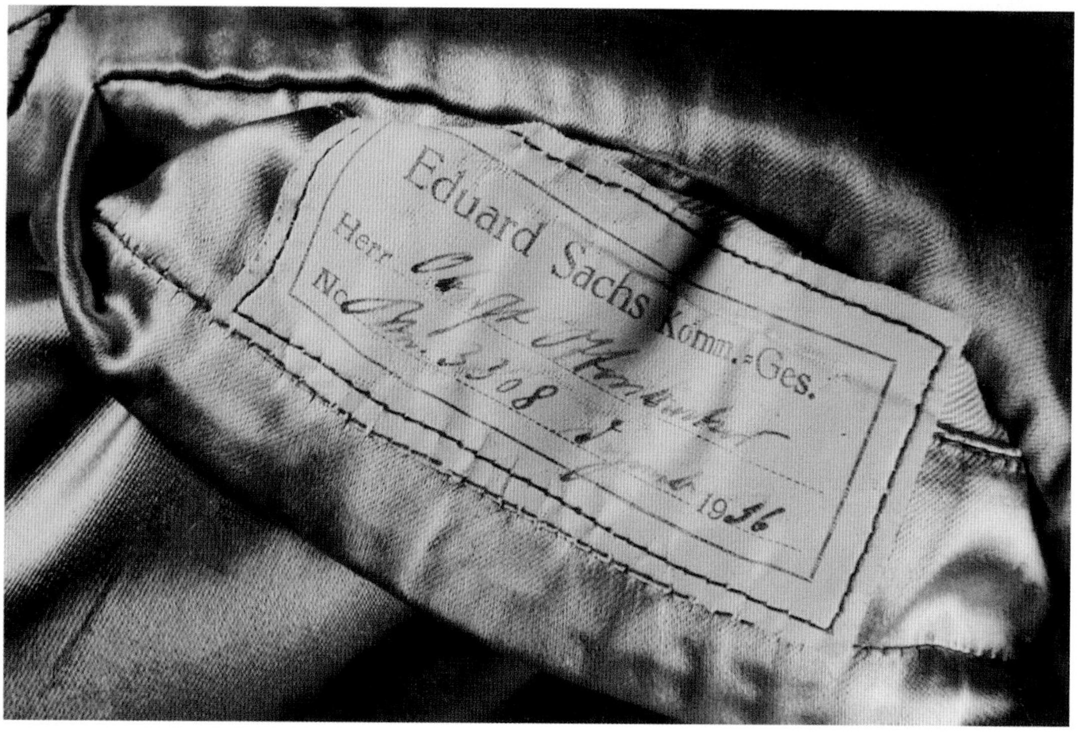
Eduard Sachs Komm.-Ges.
Herr
No

Army General Officer's Visor Hat

The Uniform of Generalmajor Erwin Rommel

This waffenrock tunic was made by Franz Heidler in Potsdam and is dated January 1937. At the time of its manufacture, Rommel was an Oberst and an instructor at the Kriegsschule in Potsdam. The trousers pictured were manufactured in Italy, and it is interesting to note that they are named to Sig. Rommel as opposed to Herr Rommel. Trousers are dated 7.10.41. *(Shea)*

FRANZ HEIDLER
POTSDAM
Herr Rommel
Datum Jan. 37. No. 1572

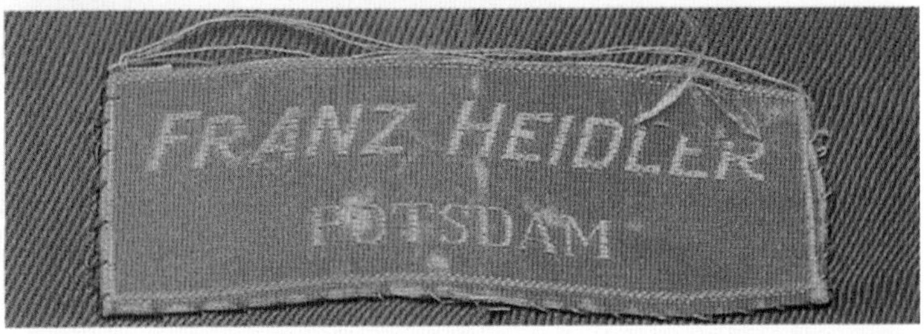
FRANZ HEIDLER
POTSDAM

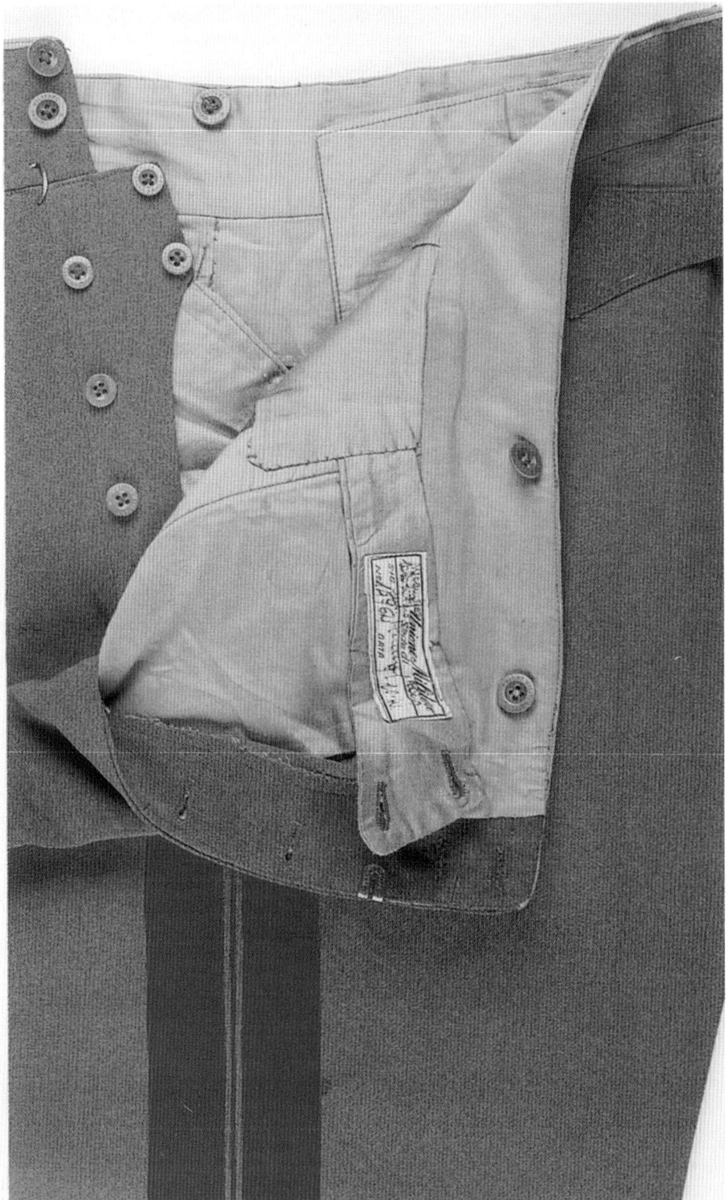

The Uniform of Generalmajor Walter Reich

This parade dress waffenrock tunic is for a Wehrmachtbeamte im Generalrang for an offical serving on the staff of the OKW or OKH. It has the white metal "HV." Walter Reich was attached to Army Group I - Berlin. Tunic is labeled Averbeck & Bröskamp in Berlin, and is dated February 1943. *(Shea and Dienna)*

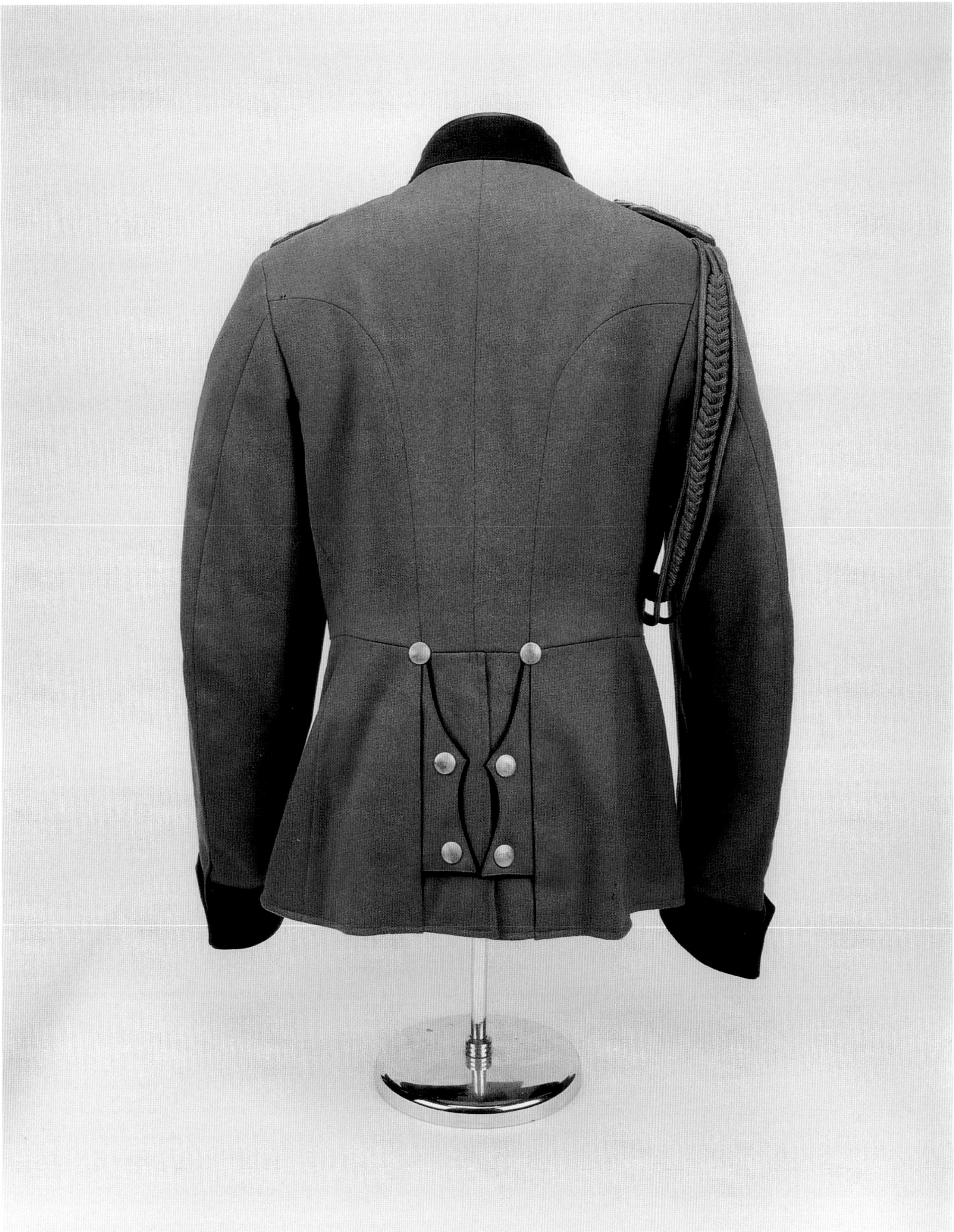

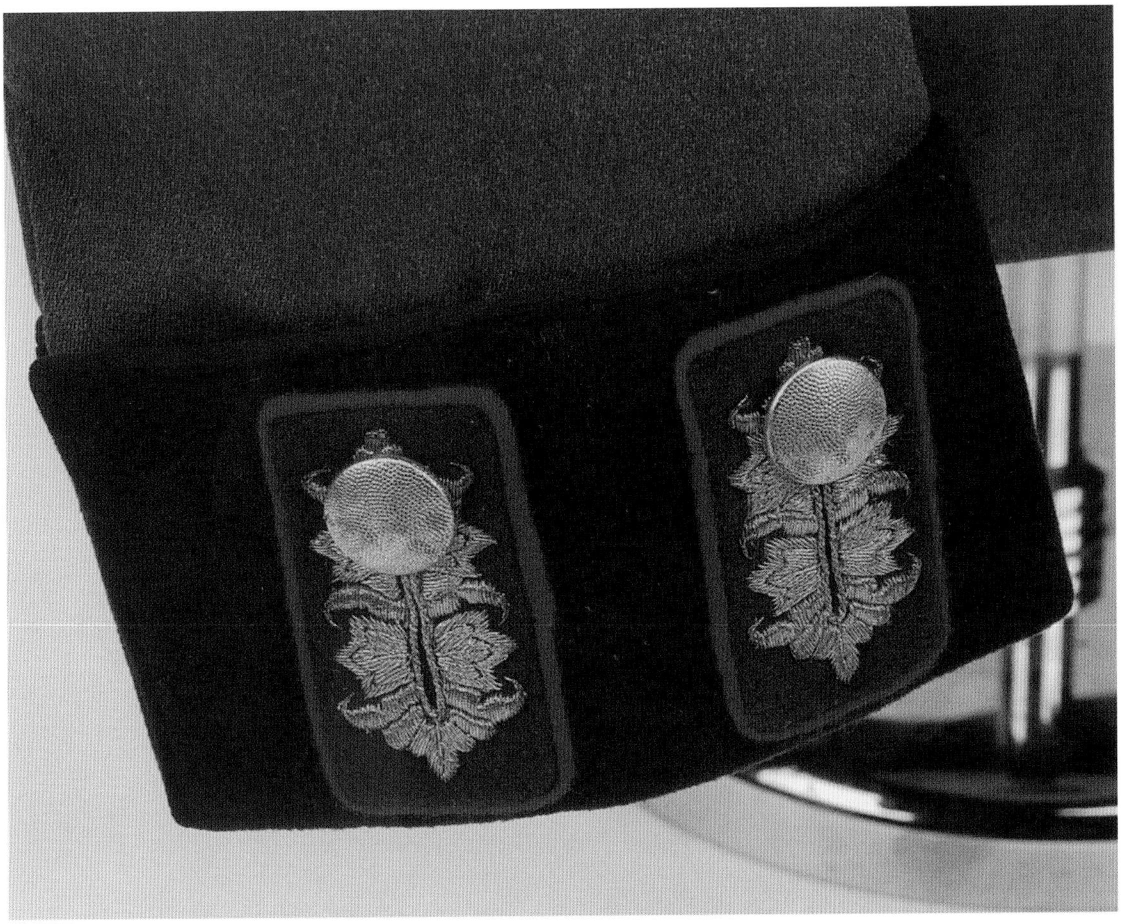

AVERBECK & BRÖSKAMP
BERLIN W.
Herr
Nr. den 194

Model 1936 Uniform of Generalveterinär Dr. Edward Richters

Tunic was manufactured by Rudolf Keller, Berlin and is dated 1941. Note veterinarian serpent insignia on shoulder boards. Note "Dr.KR" initials in hat (Klaus was Richters' proper first name). *(Shea)*

1939
1939

D
K
R

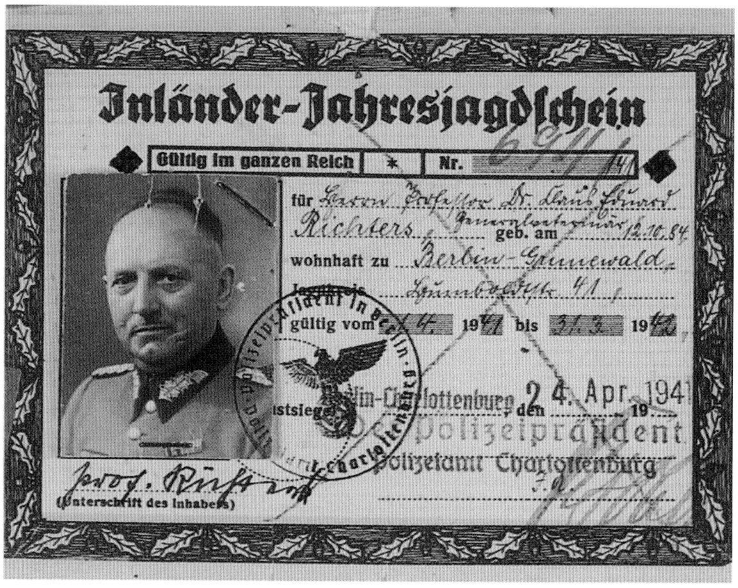
Inländer-Jahresjagdschein
Gültig im ganzen Reich
Nr.
für
geb. am
wohnhaft zu
gültig vom
bis
den
24. Apr. 1941
Polizeipräsident
Polizeiamt Charlottenburg
(Unterschrift des Inhabers)

Model 1936 Uniform of Generalmajor (Generalrichter) Dr. A. Grün

Tunic was manufactured by L.H. Berger, Collani & Co., Berlin and is dated 9.10.44. Wine red waffenfarbe denotes judiciary corps. Grün was a high ranking judge whose job was to review the results of all military tribunals. *(Shea)*

L.H.Berger,Collani & Co.
Berlin SW 68 Friedrichstraße 210
HERRN Dr. A. Grün
9.10.44 Nr. 384

Standard Army General's Overcoat of General der Panzertruppe Walther Nehring

Nehring held the Knight's Cross with Oak Leaves and Swords, and served as the commander of the Afrikakorps in 1942. He later fought brilliantly in Russia for over two years. Overcoat has Nehring's North African campaign cuff title. Tailor's label is from Armeemarinehaus, Berlin = Charlottenburg 2, and is dated 15.1.37. *(Shea)*

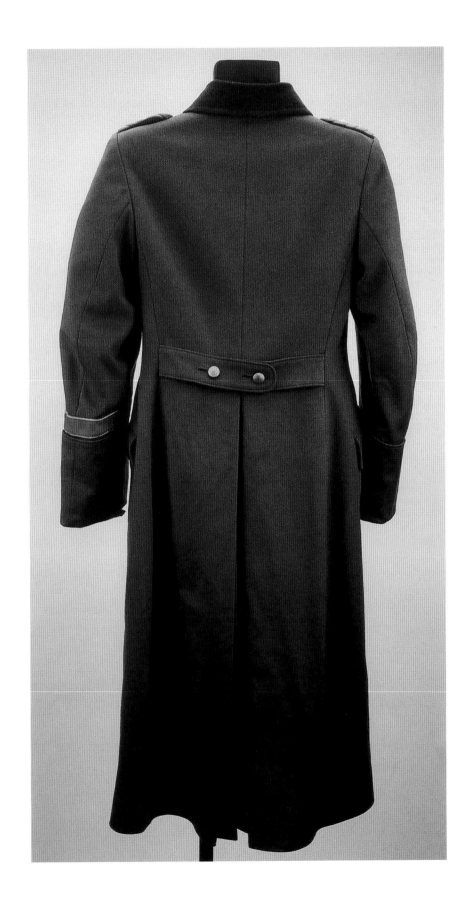

AFRIKA

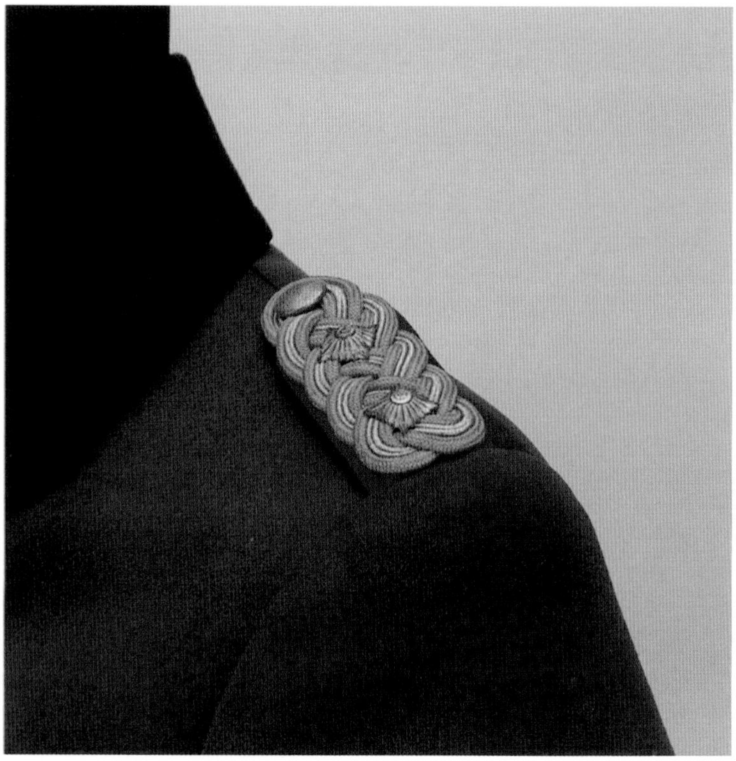

Armeemarinehaus
Berlin=Charlottenburg 2
Herr

The Walking Out Dress Uniform of an Army Infantry Leutnant

This is a tailor made example of the standard German Army officer's service uniform. The tunic is shown with the brown leather officer's belt and cross strap and with the brocade parade dress belt. The Army officer's dress dagger is also displayed as worn.

Army officer's cap piped in white for Infantry.

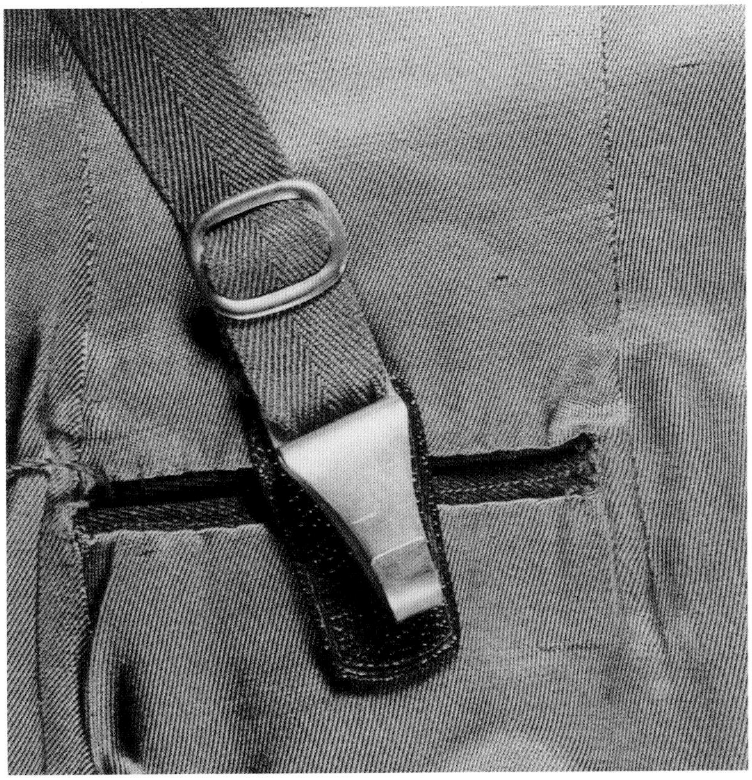

Dagger hanger and opening for hanger inside of coat.

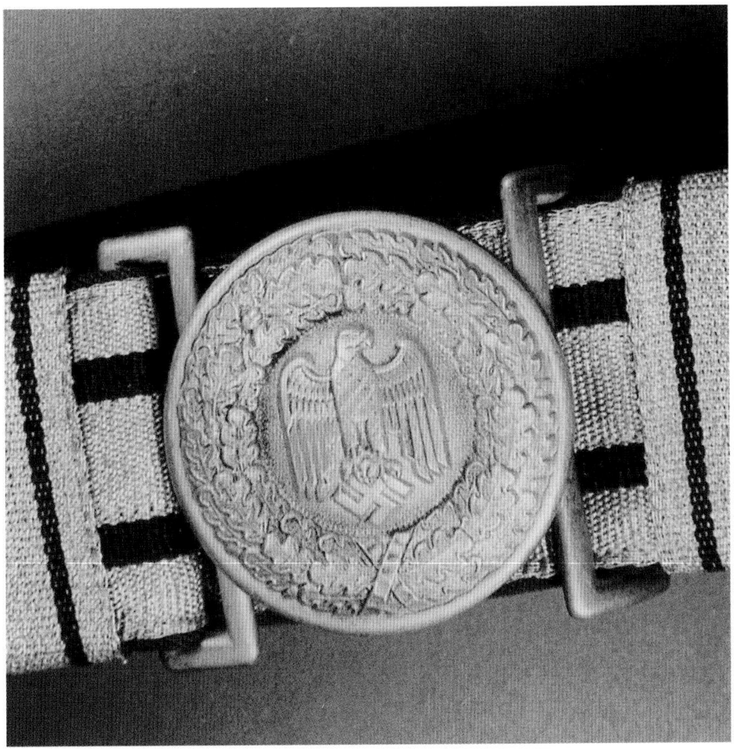

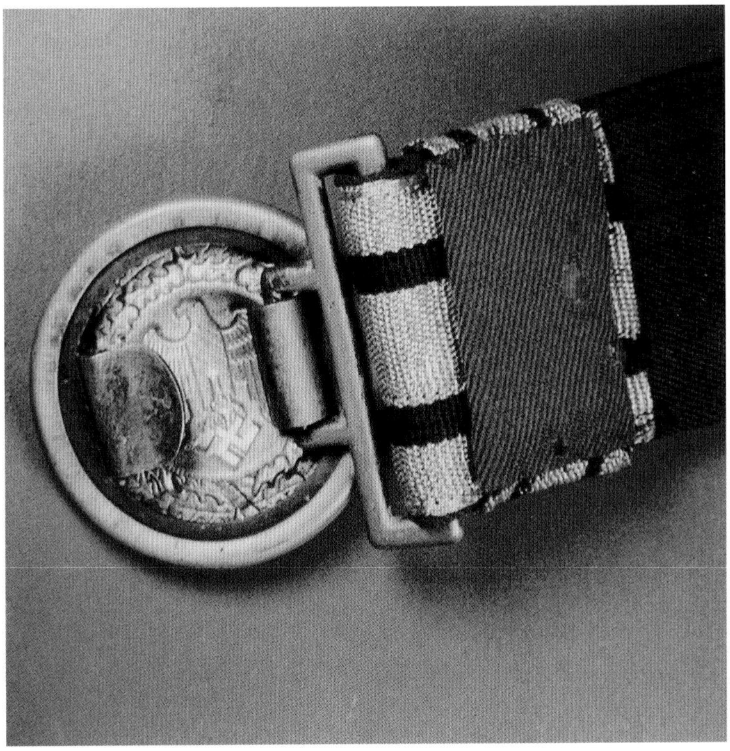

Detail of Army officer's brocade dress belt and buckle.

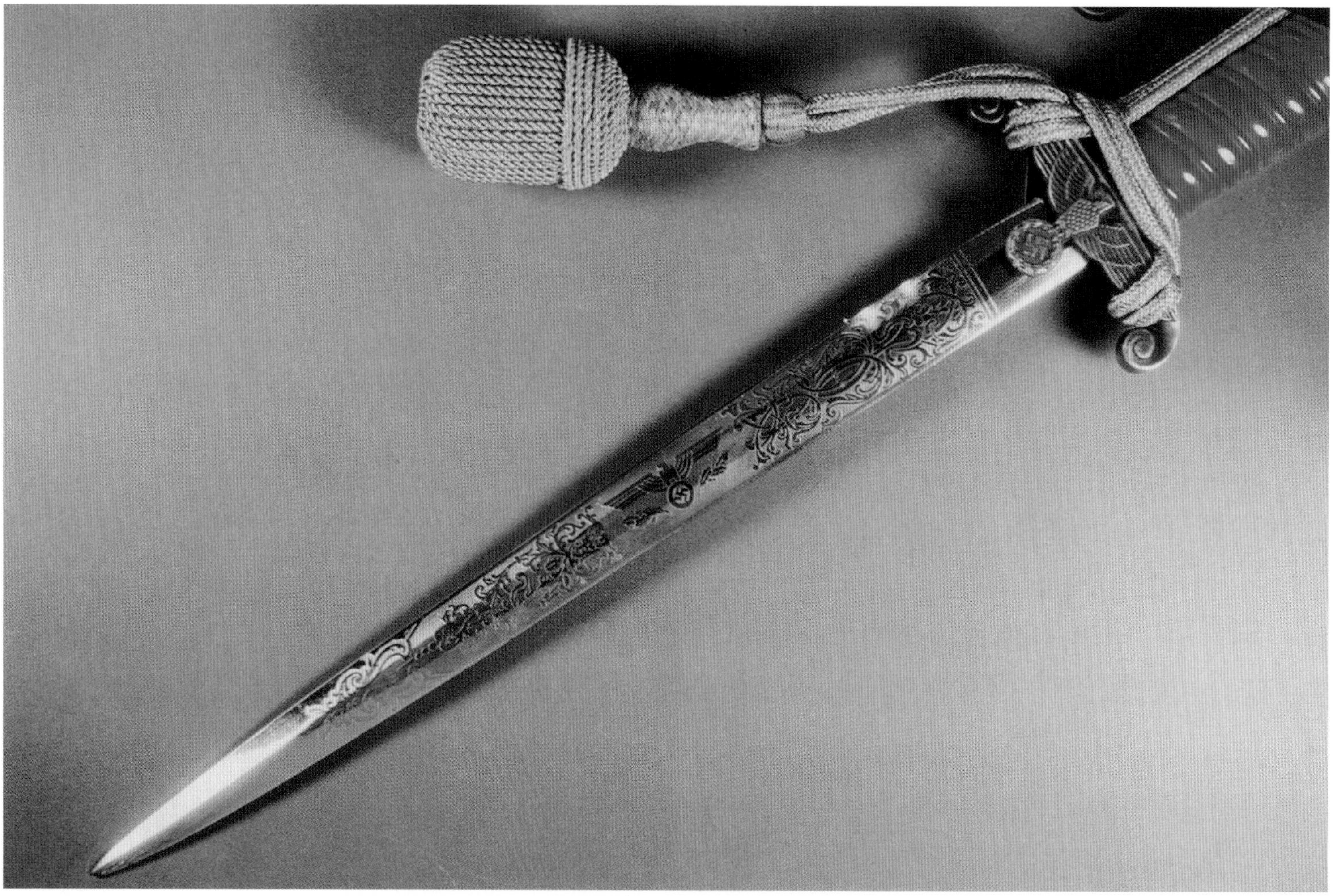

Extremely high quality Army officer's dress dagger with etched blade by Emil Voos.

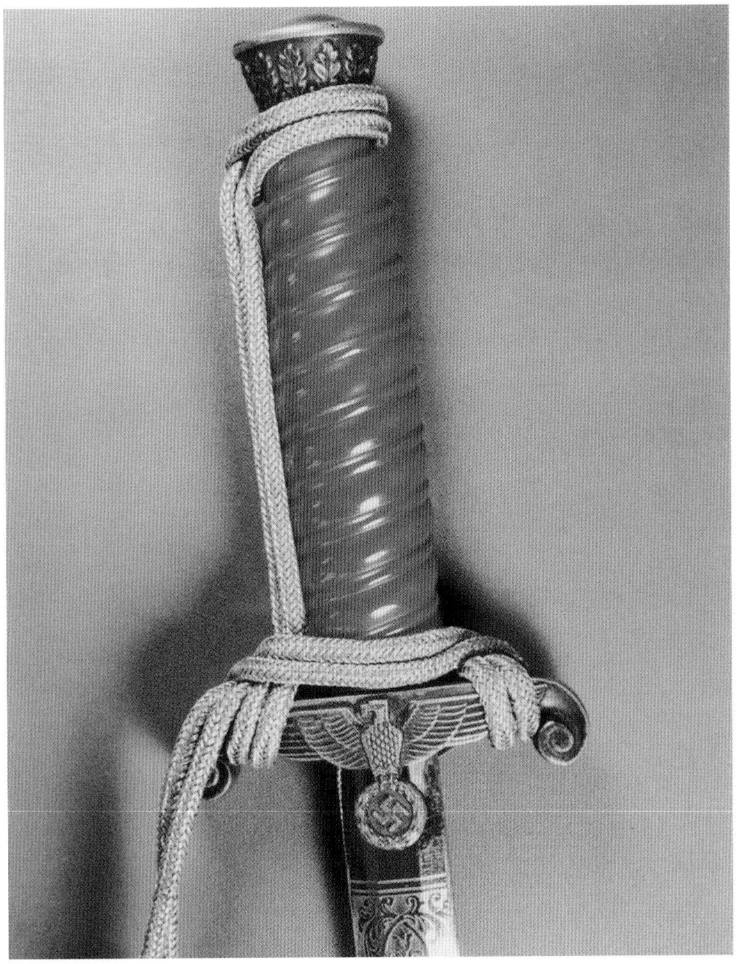

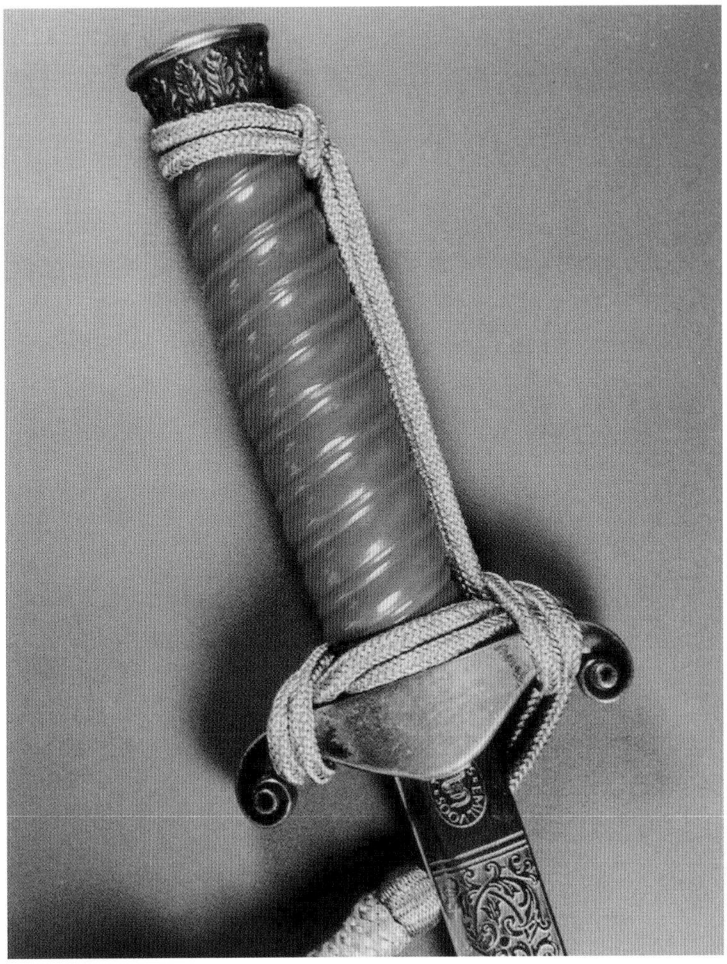

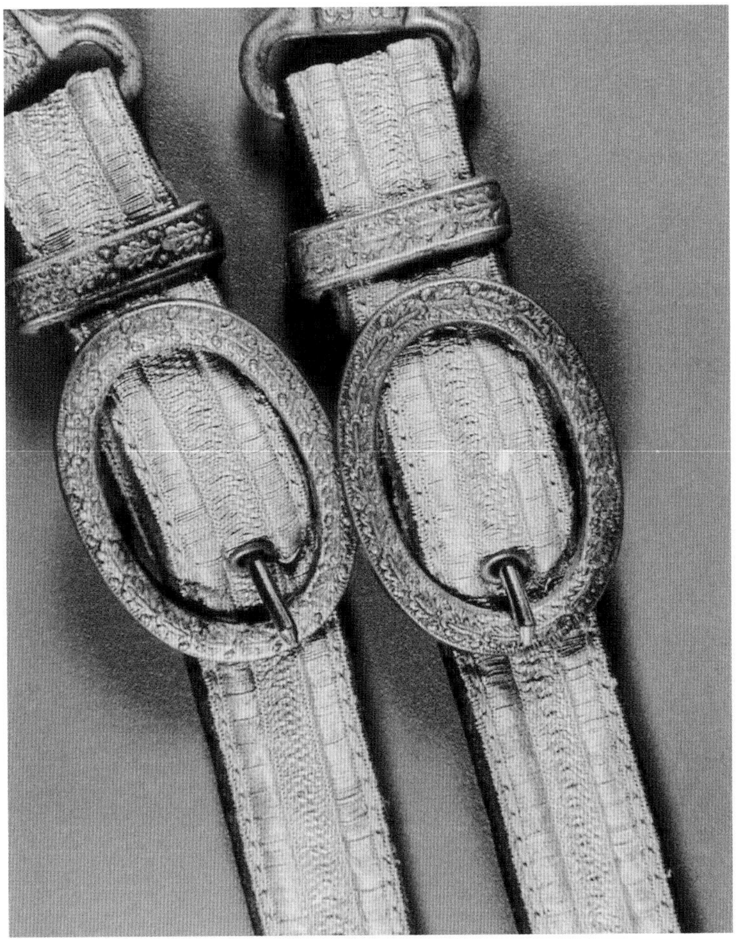

Left and above: Detail of fittings on unusually high quality dagger hangers.

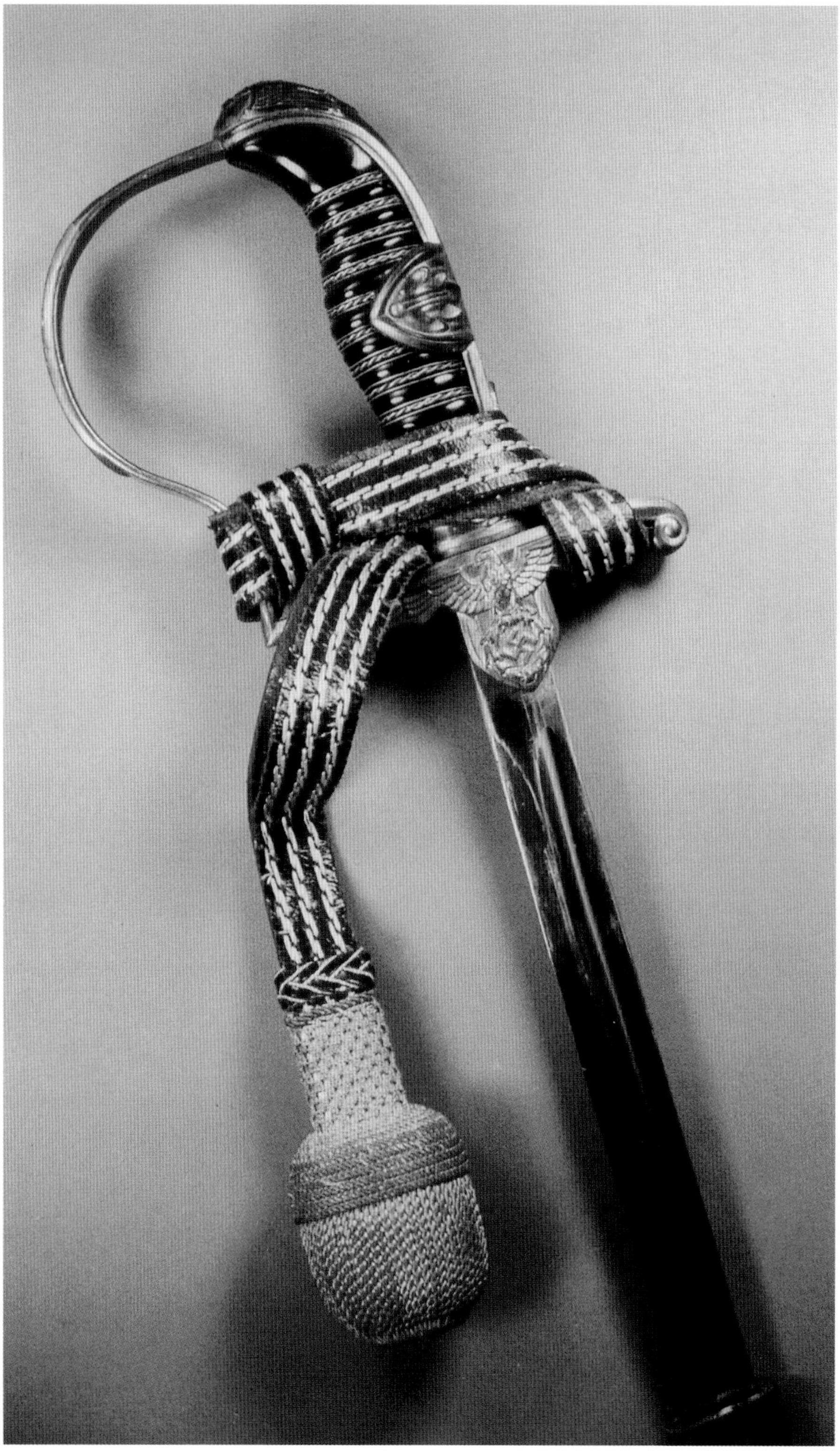

German Army officer's dress sword and troddle.

Elastolin toy soldiers of the period depicted in Army uniforms.

The Panzer Officer's Special Black Uniform of Rudolf Gerhardt

This style of uniform was worn by all ranks serving in armored fighting vehicles. This tailor made example was worn by the commander of the Panzer Lehr Regiment, Rudolf Gerhardt. Gerhardt took command of the regiment in November of 1943. The coat features unusual, non-standard collar tabs.

AFRIKA

SIZE 36

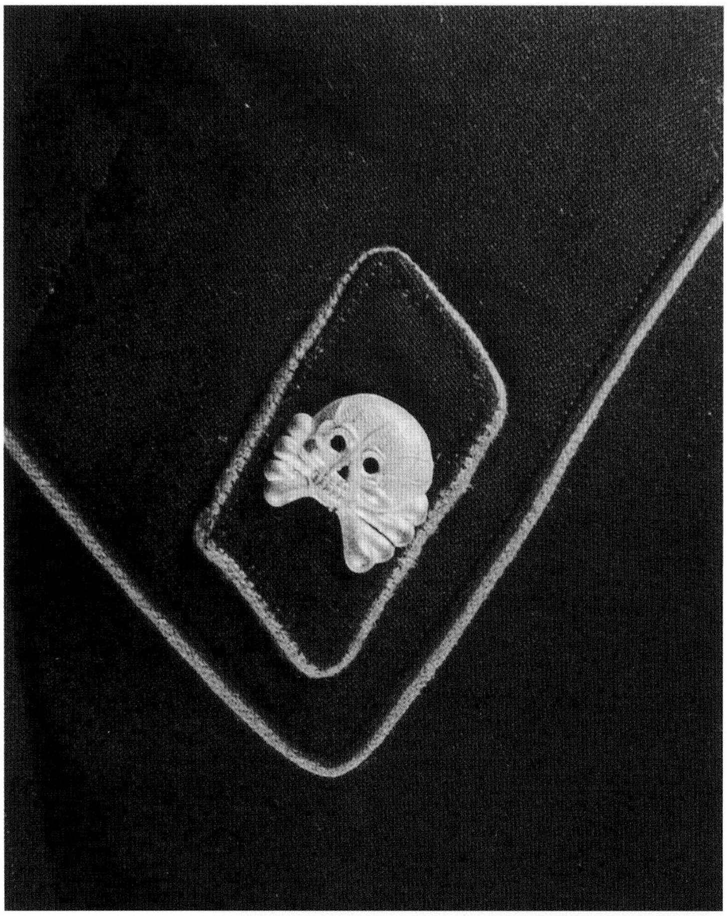

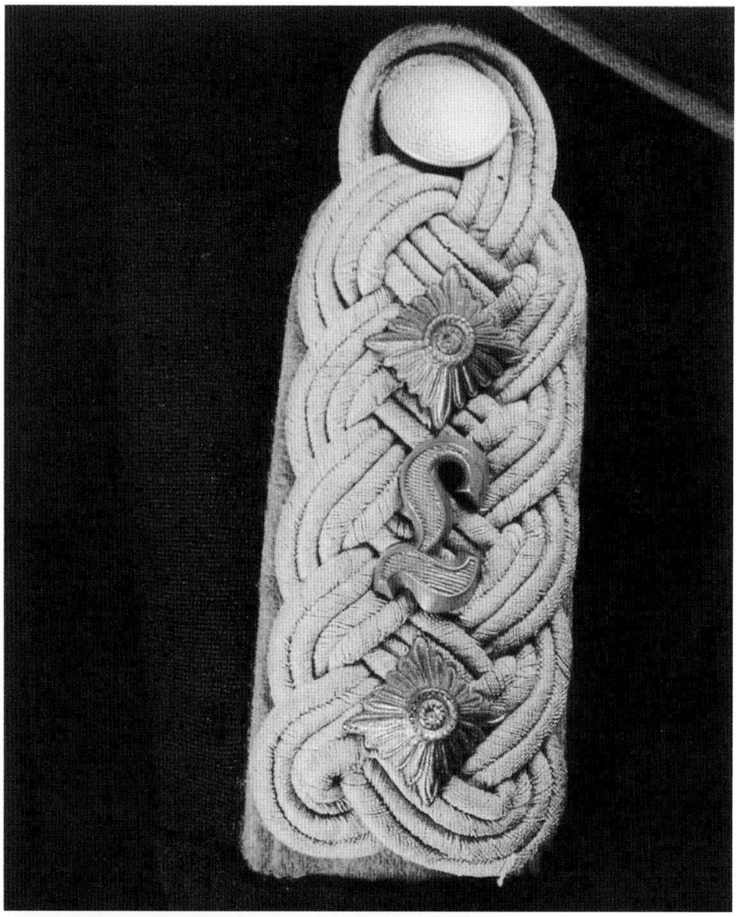

AFRIKA

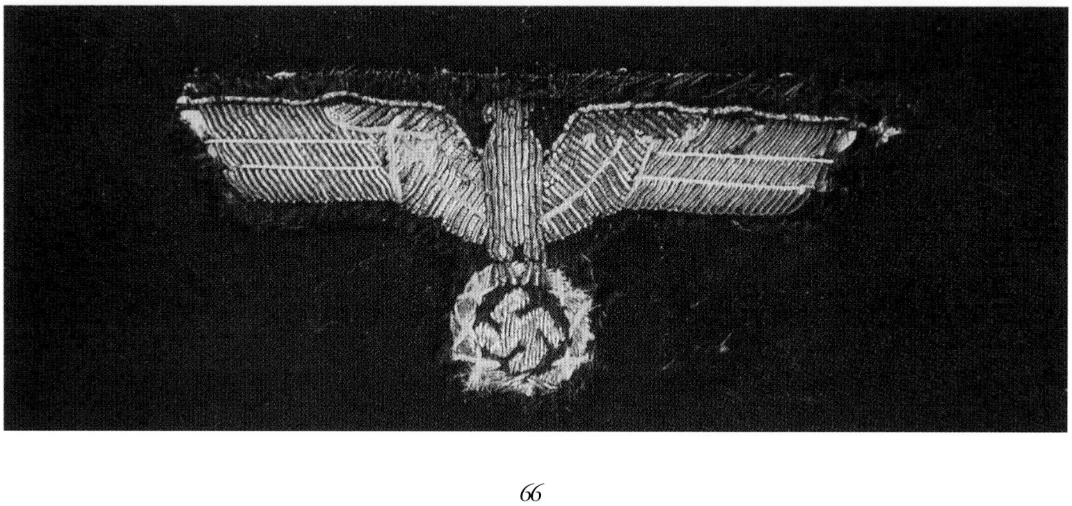

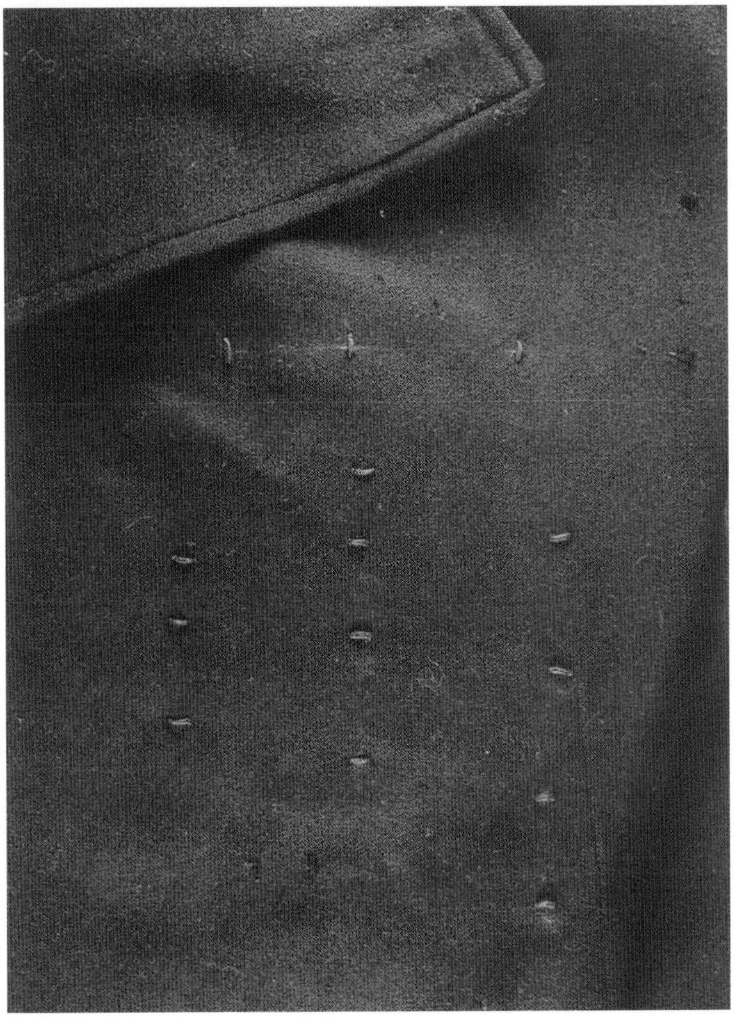

Detail of the loops for decorations on the left chest.

Markings inside the breeches.

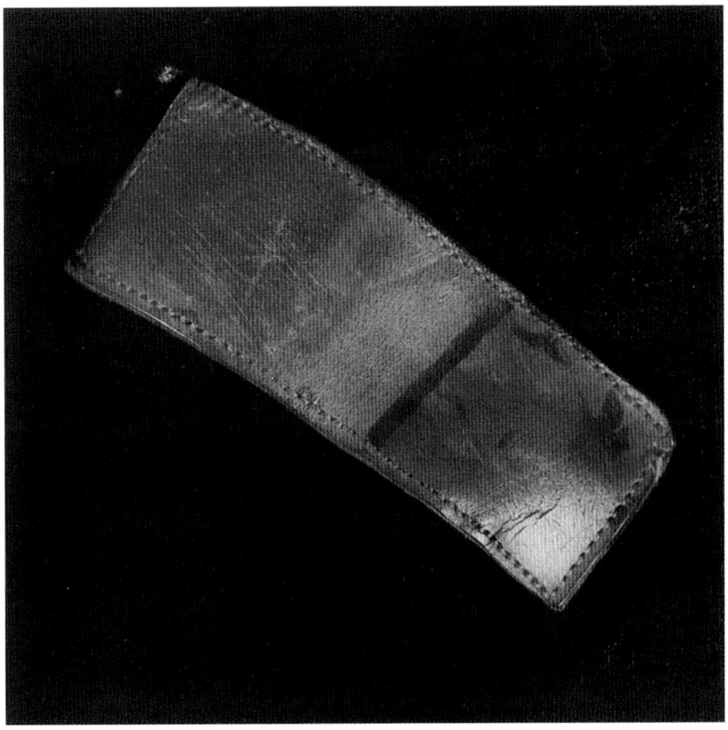

Leather reinforcement on inner leg of breeches.

A Panzer officer on parade wearing the black uniform and beret.

The black feldmütze with red soutach for artillery.

The black Panzer beret was a distinctive feature of the black uniform. This is the officer's version.

Panzer officer's visor cap.

The Panzer NCO's Special Black Uniform

This example was worn by Gustav Muller. Note the addition of red fabric behind the eyes of the skull on the collar tabs.

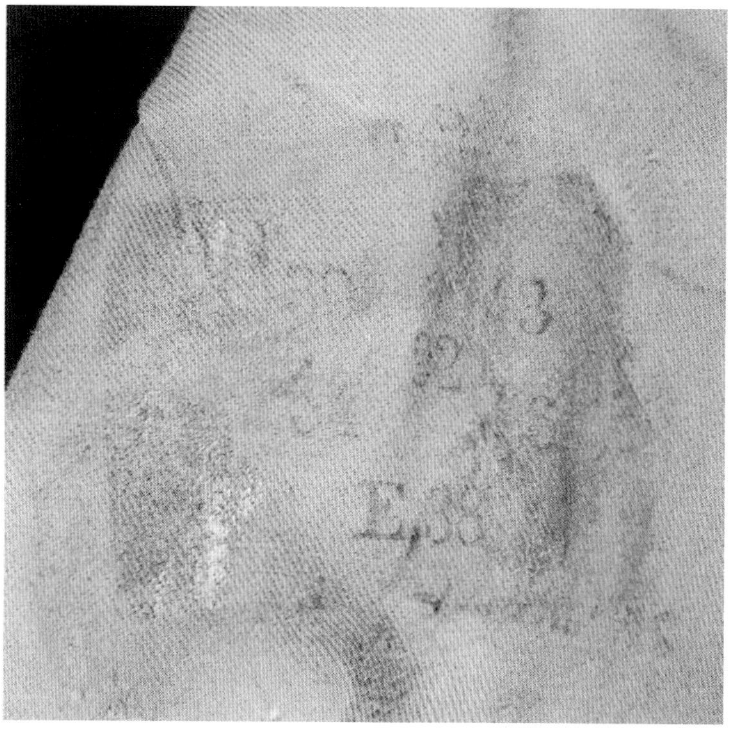

Right: Gustav Muller wearing his black Panzer uniform.

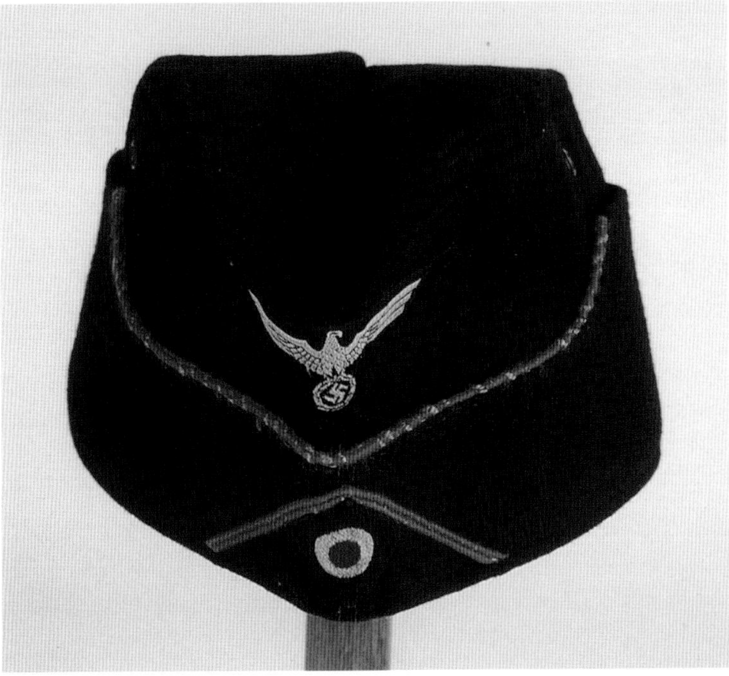

The black Panzer feldmütze for EM / NCO.

M-43 field cap for EM / NCO Panzer troops.

Black Panzer beret for EM / NCO.

Panzer Officer's Service Dress Tunic

This example is an early war piece with scalloped pockets, dark green collar and French cuffs. Insignia on the shoulder boards indicates the 11th Panzer Division. The coat has a Krim (Crimea) Shield on the left sleeve and a Tank Destroyer strip on the right sleeve. *(Matthew Reinert, MHS)*

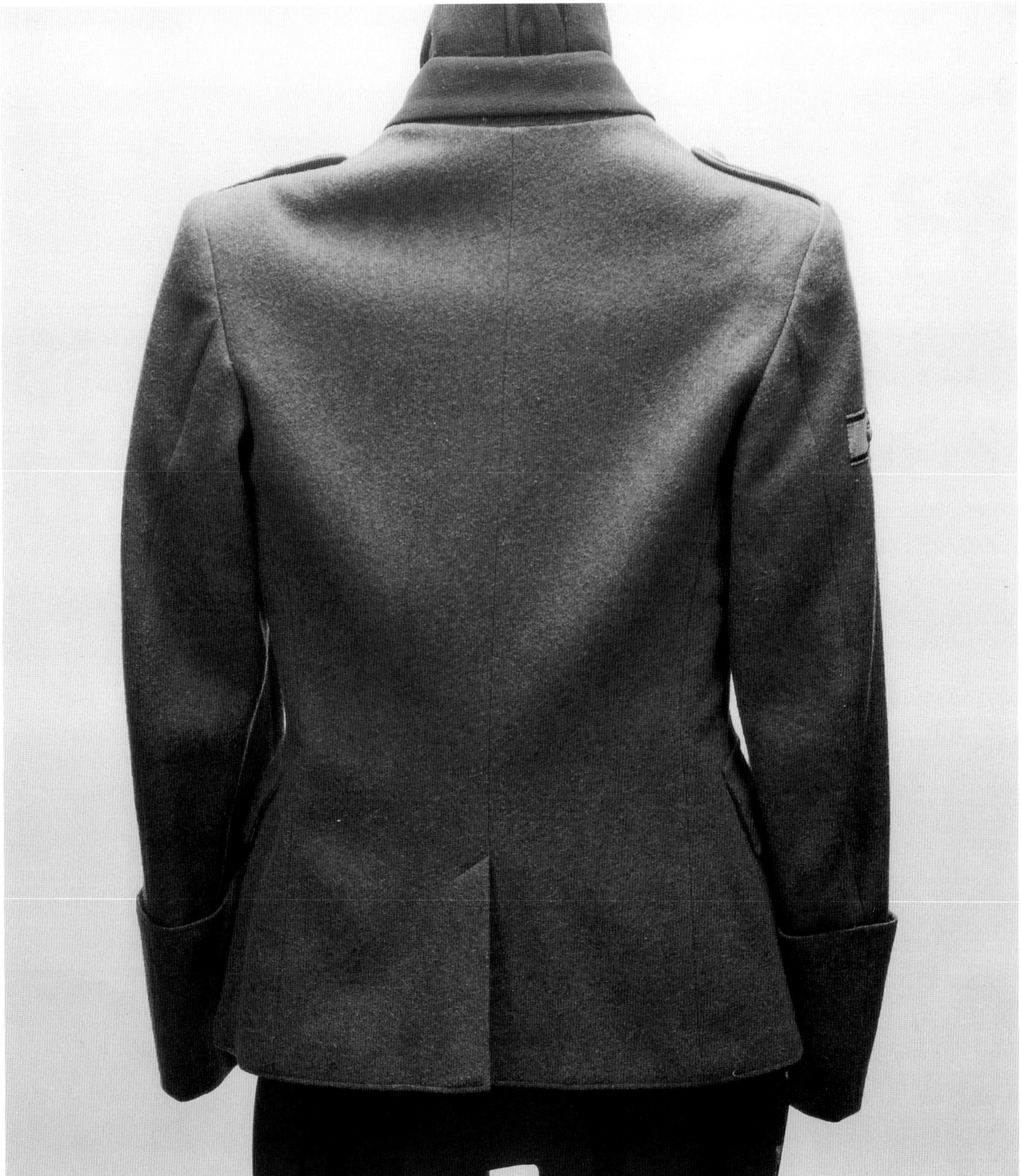

1941
1942
KRIM

Enlisted Ranks Tropical Green Tunic "Afrikakorps"

This tropical tunic has the green waffenfarbe of a Mountain Jäger unit. Note the Edelweiss and Afrikakorps sleeve band on the right sleeve. The tunic is displayed with the standard Afrikakorps issue webbed belt and buckle. *(Matthew Reinert, MHS)*

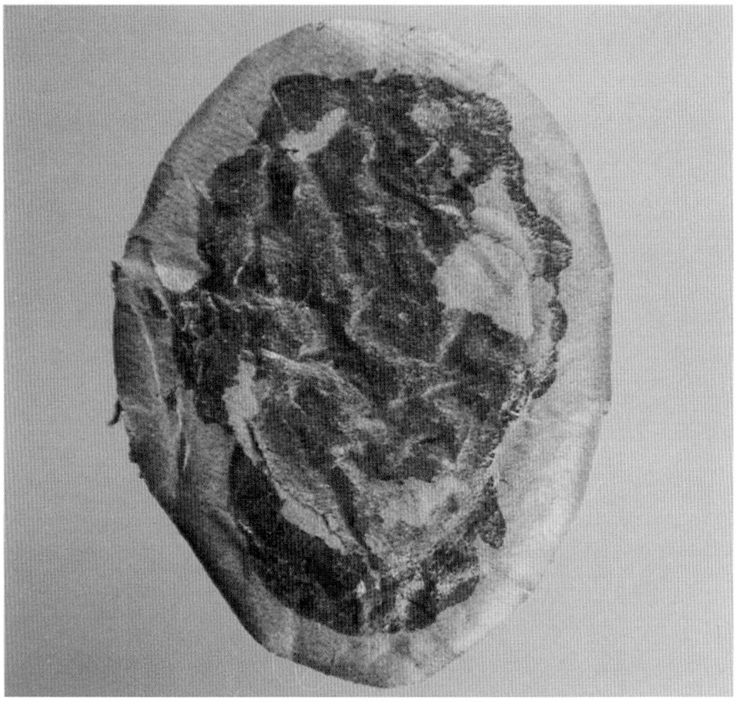

Detail of an original Edelweiss insignia as worn by mountain troops.

2

Luftwaffe

The Service Tunic "Tuchrock" of a Luftwaffe Generalleutnant

This style of open collar tunic was introduced in March of 1937. It is displayed with the General Officer's brown leather belt and gold buckle. The belt is backed with blue wool.

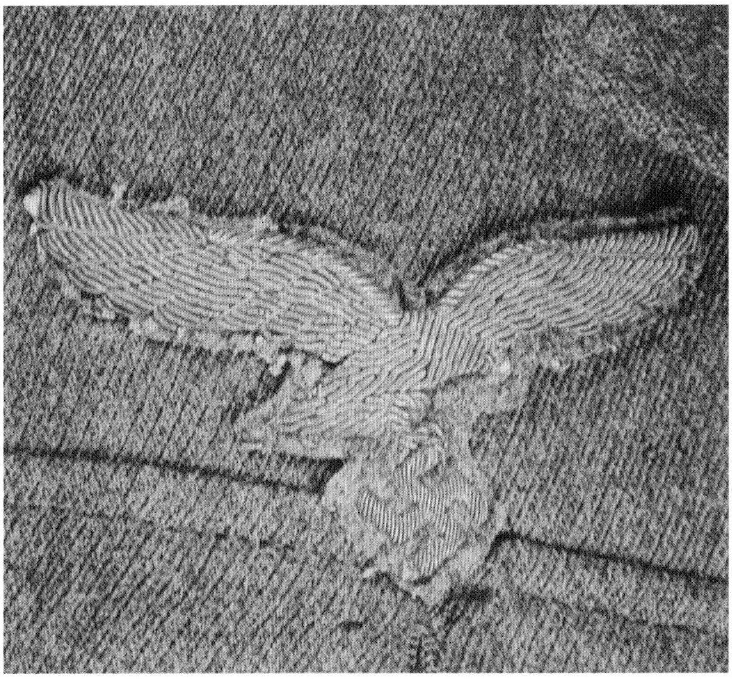

Detail of dagger hanger and opening inside of tunic for the dagger hanger to pass through.

Reverse of belt displaying the blue wool backing.

Luftwaffe Generalleutnant's Overcoat

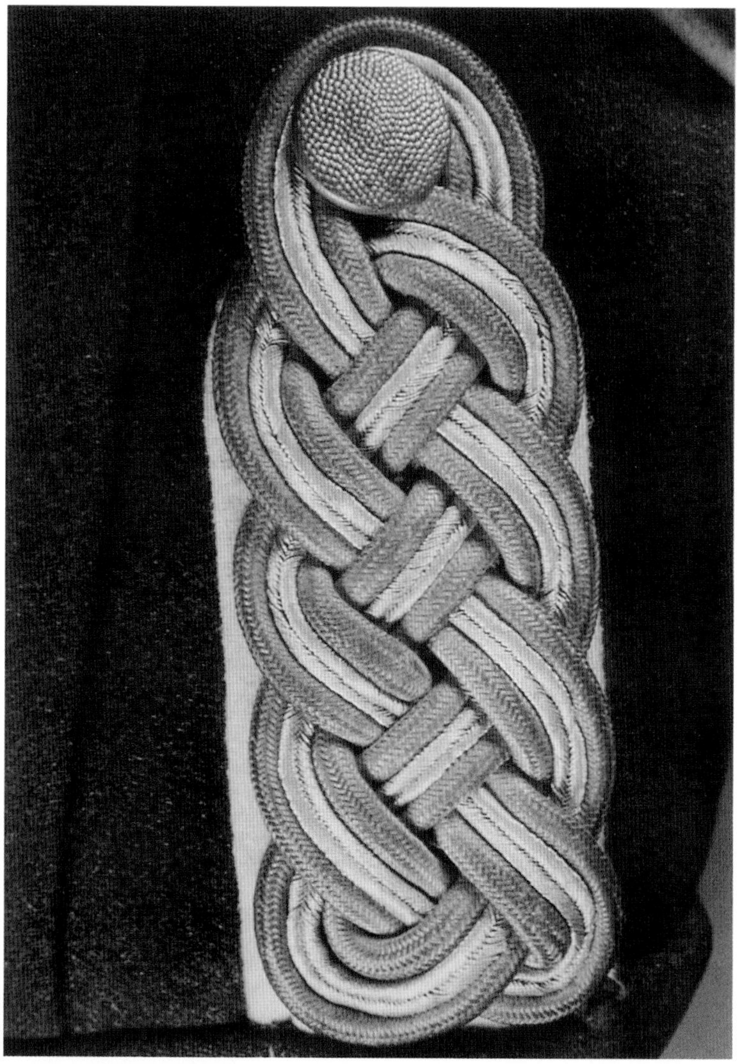

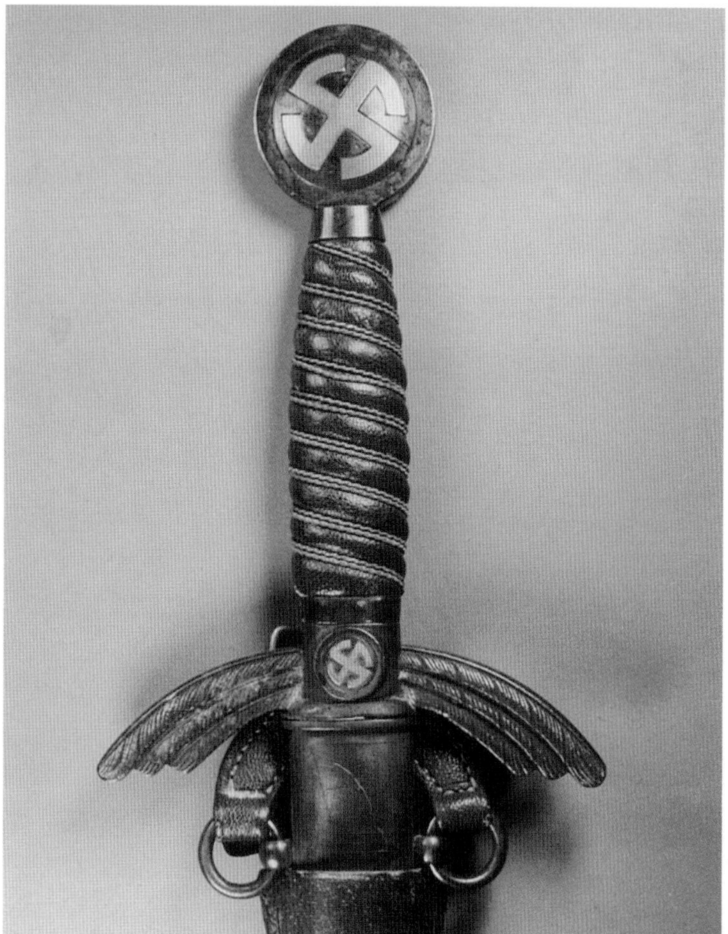

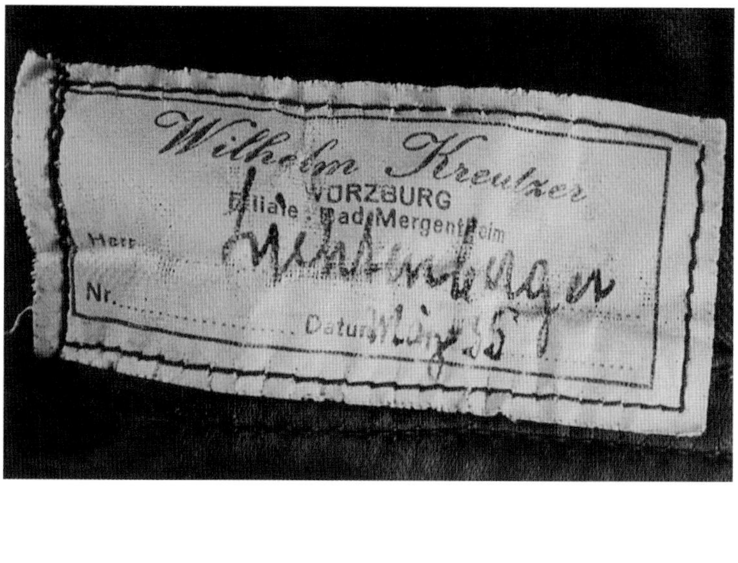

Left: The hilt of a Luftwaffe Officer's Sword.

Luftwaffe General Officer's Visor Cap

Uniform of General der Flieger Stefan Fröhlich

This uniform was manufactured in March 1938, by the firm of Wiebag in Wien, when Fröhlich was an Oberst. It was later upgraded as he was promoted. Fröhlich won the Knight's Cross on 4.7.40 as Generalmajor and Kommandeur of KG 76. He later served in Africa on Rommel's staff. *(Shea)*

AFRIKA

WR. BKLDGS. HDLS. u. BED. ART. A.G.
Wiebag
WIEN I.
STUBENRING 1 KRIEGSMINISTERIUM

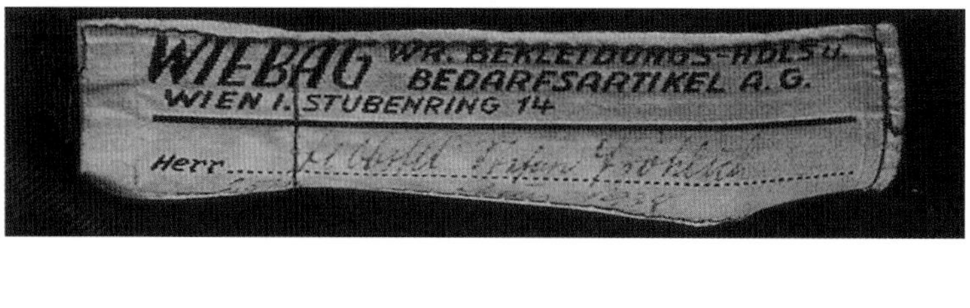
WIEBAG WR. BEKLEIDUNGS-HDLS u.
BEDARFSARTIKEL A.G.
WIEN I. STUBENRING 14
Herr

General der Flieger Stefan Fröhlich.

Luftwaffe Formal Evening Dress Uniform

Uniform rank insignia denotes Generalmajor. Uniform was manufactured by Averbeck & Bröskamp in Berlin. *(Shea)*

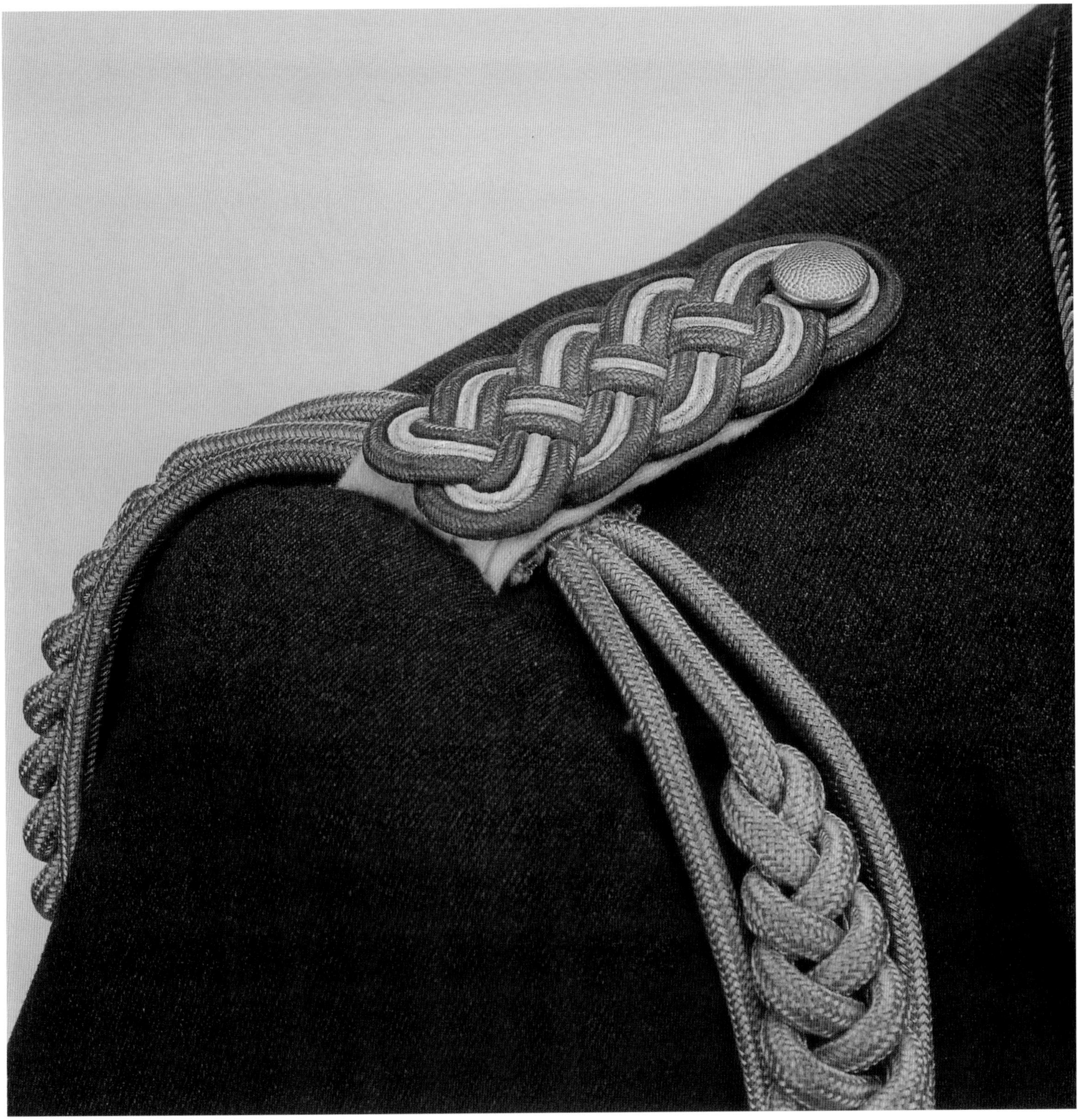

The Service Tunic "Tuchrock" of a Luftwaffe Oberleutnant of Flight

This officer's uniform is piped in yellow, indicating he is a flying officer. It is displayed with a very interesting adjutant's aiguillette with metal rings which are engraved with the names of the previous holders of the position. The tunic has a Pilot's Badge, Reconnaissance War Flight Bar, and Silver Wound Badge. Also shown is an early style black officer's belt with "droop tail" eagle and a first pattern flyer's dagger.

Hermann Schiedung
GOTHA
SCHÄFERSTR. 18

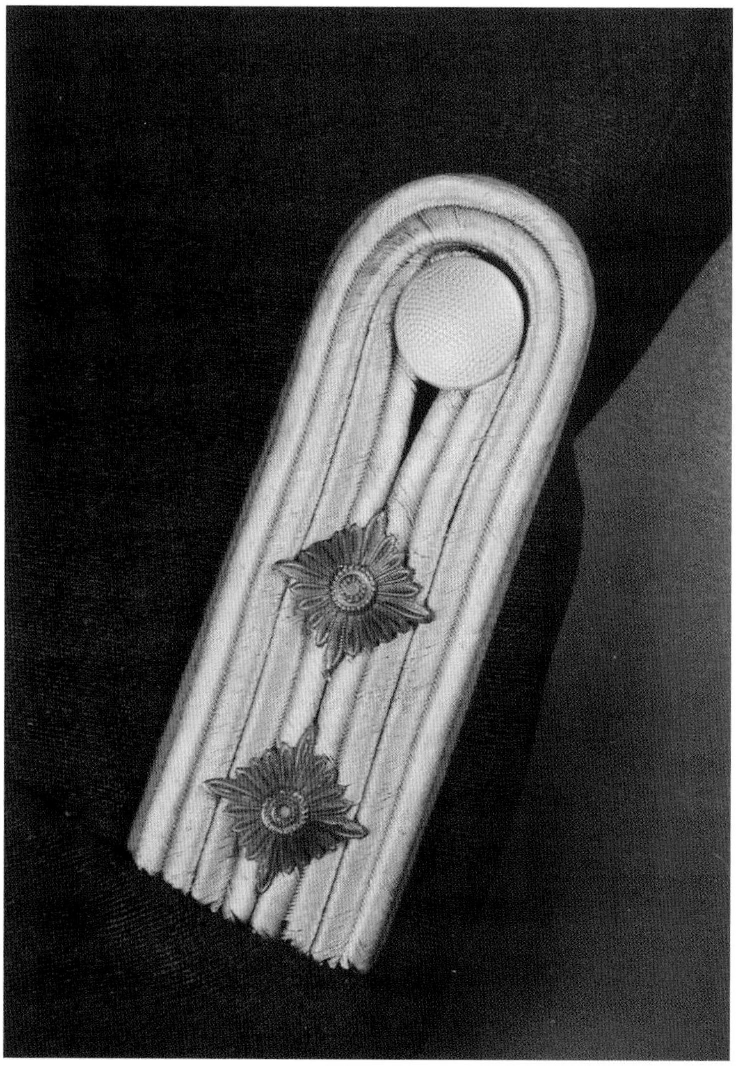

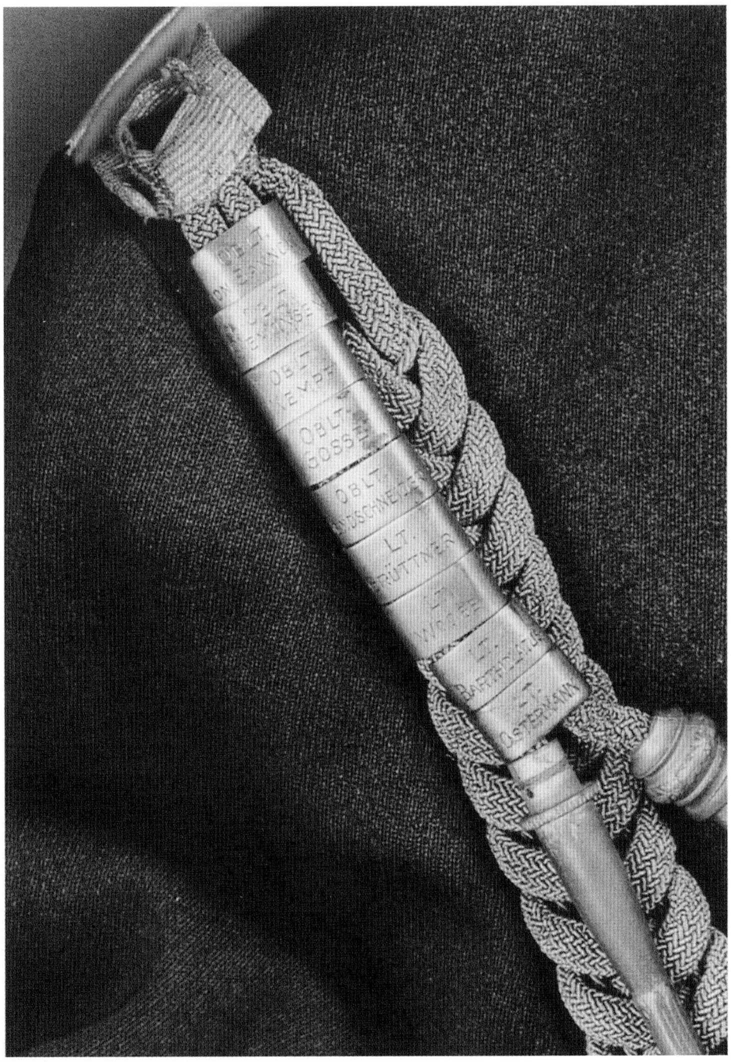

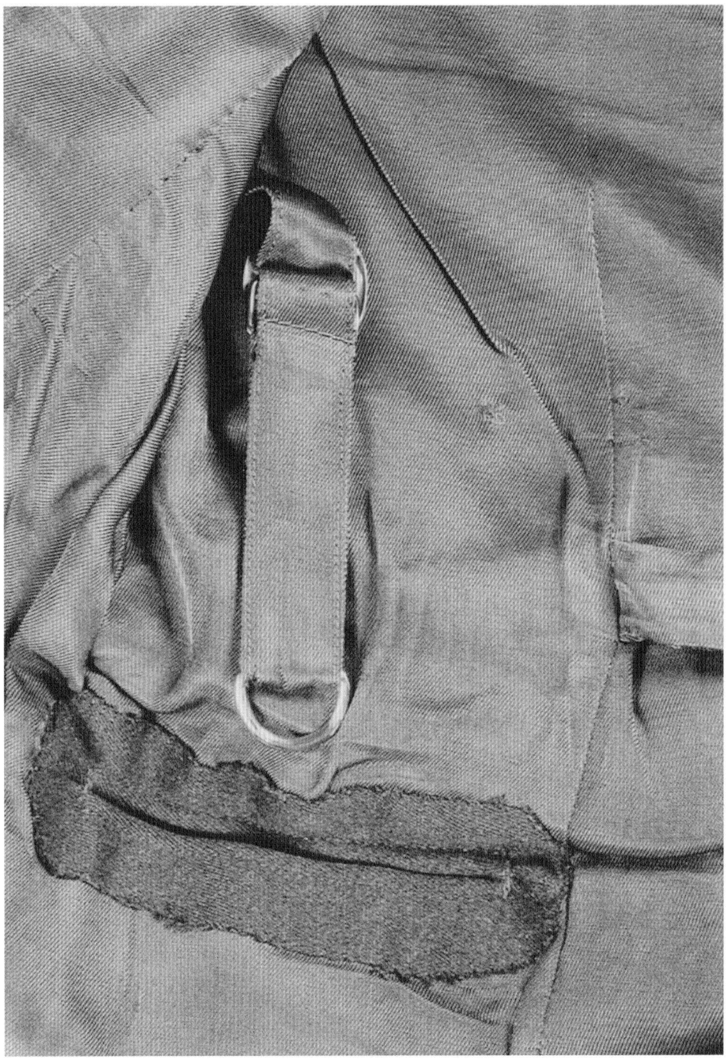

Dagger hanger and opening for same inside of tunic.

Detail of early Luftwaffe officer's belt buckle.

High quality Luftwaffe officer's hat made by EREL.

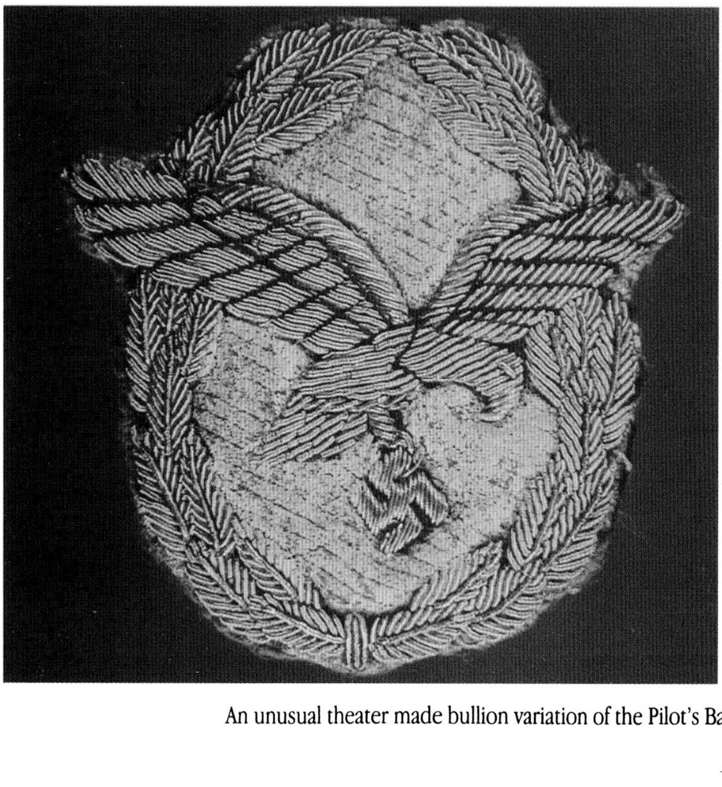

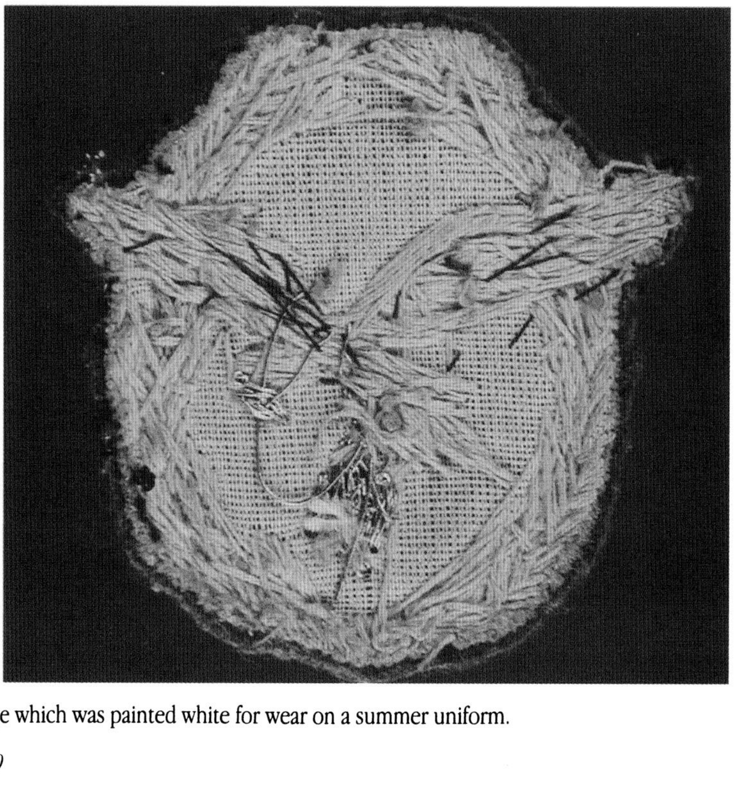

An unusual theater made bullion variation of the Pilot's Badge which was painted white for wear on a summer uniform.

Luftwaffe flag pole top.

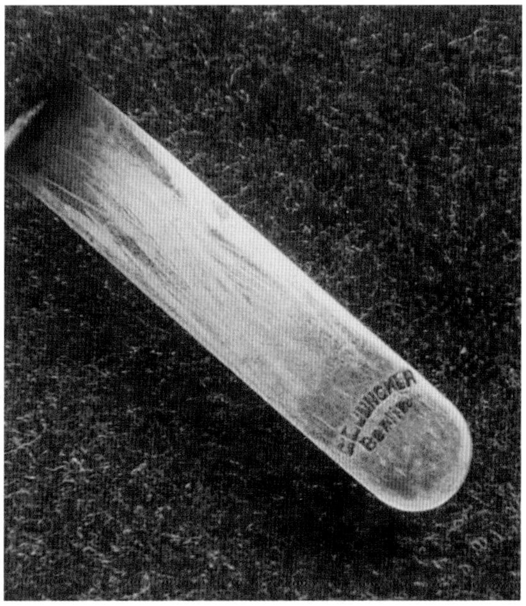

Left: The Luftwaffe Standard Bearer's Gorget.
Above: Maker's mark of C. E. Juncker on the gorget.

Luftwaffe Stabsfeldwebel's Service Tunic of the Regiment General Göring

General Göring

General Göring

General G

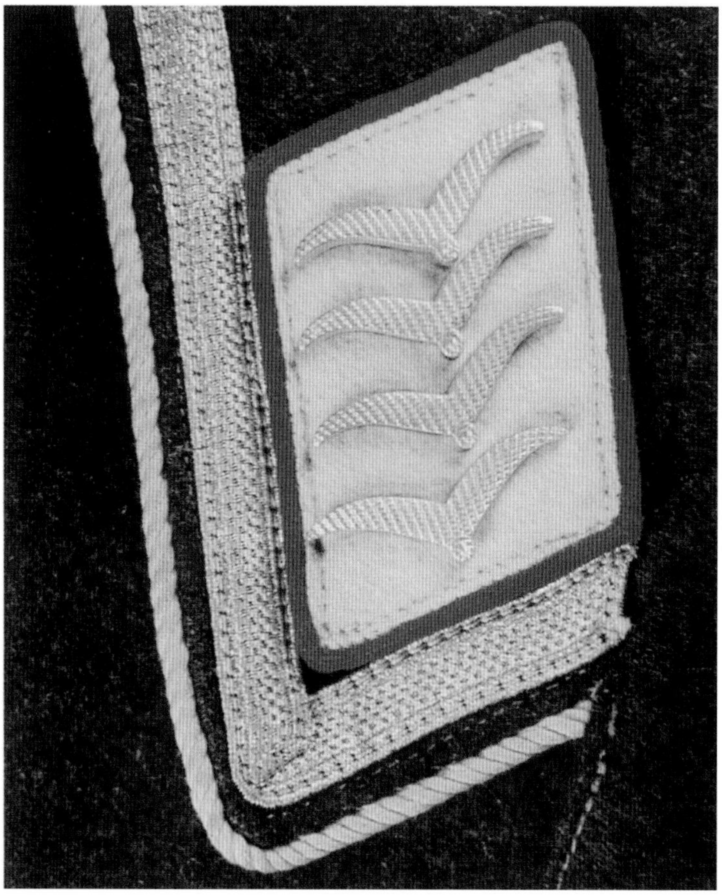

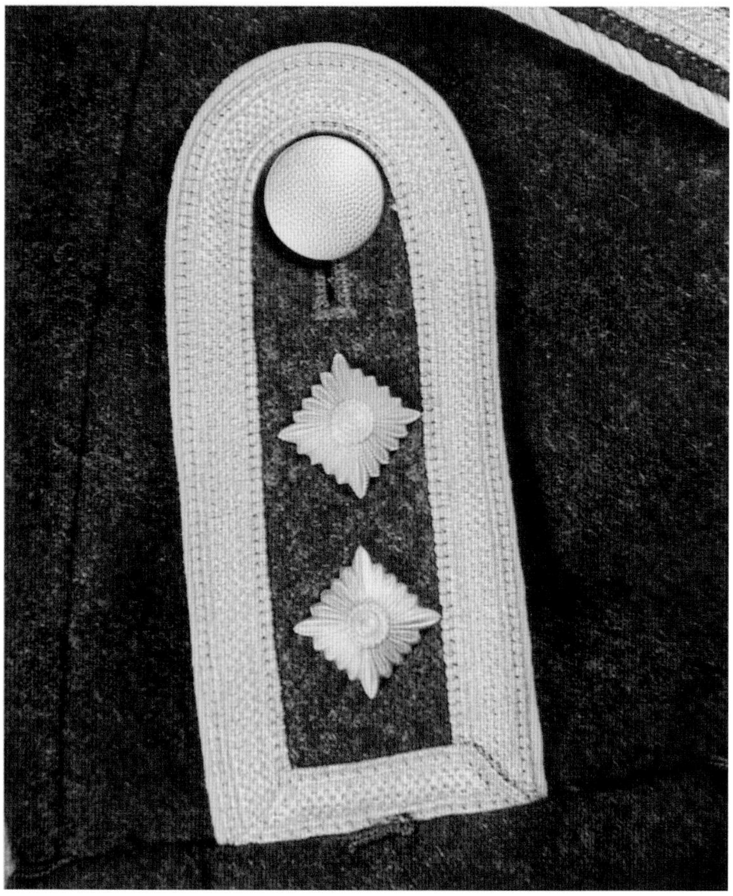

Elastolin toy soldiers of the period in Luftwaffe uniforms.

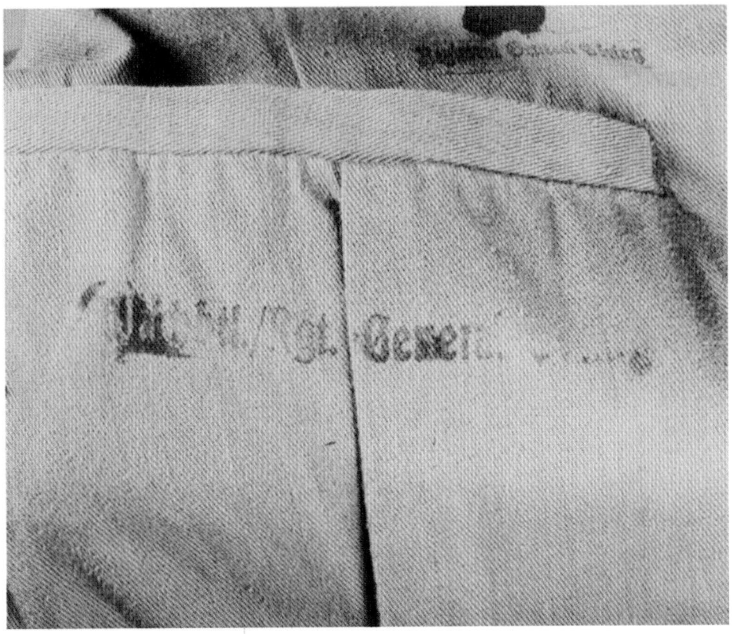

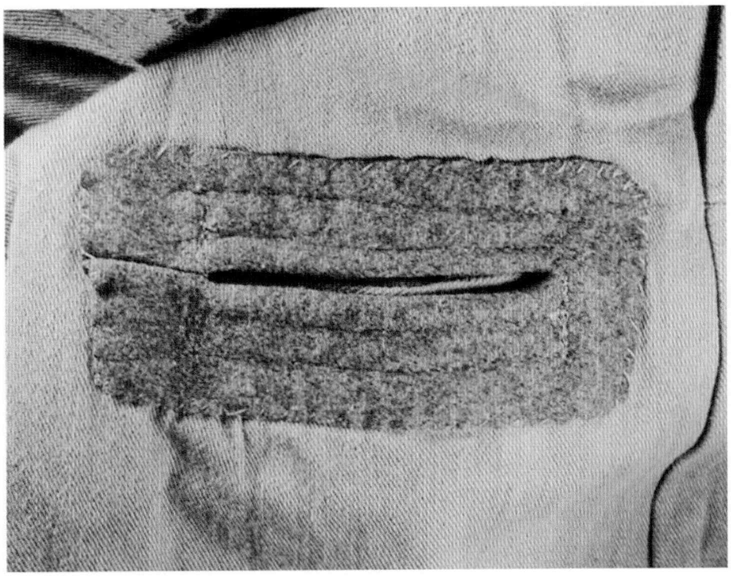

Opening inside tunic for the dagger hanger to pass through.

NCO ranks visor cap piped in white, indicating the General Göring Division.

Luftwaffe Flying Service Blouse - "Fliegerbluse" - of a Medical Feldwebel

This uniform features a marksman's lanyard, Krete cuff title and an Afrika cuff title. It is shown here with the standard service belt and dress bayonet.

KRETA
AFRIKA

Size 35

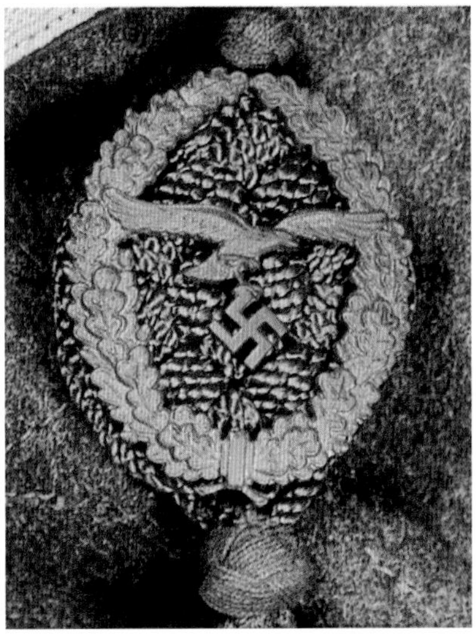

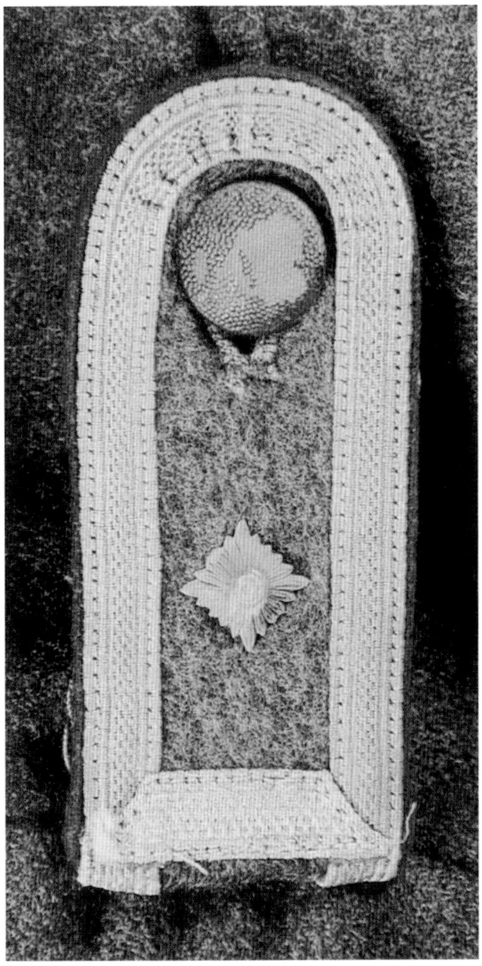

Luftwaffe Medical NCO visor cap.

3

Kriegsmarine

Uniforms of Admiral Karl-Jesko von Puttkamer

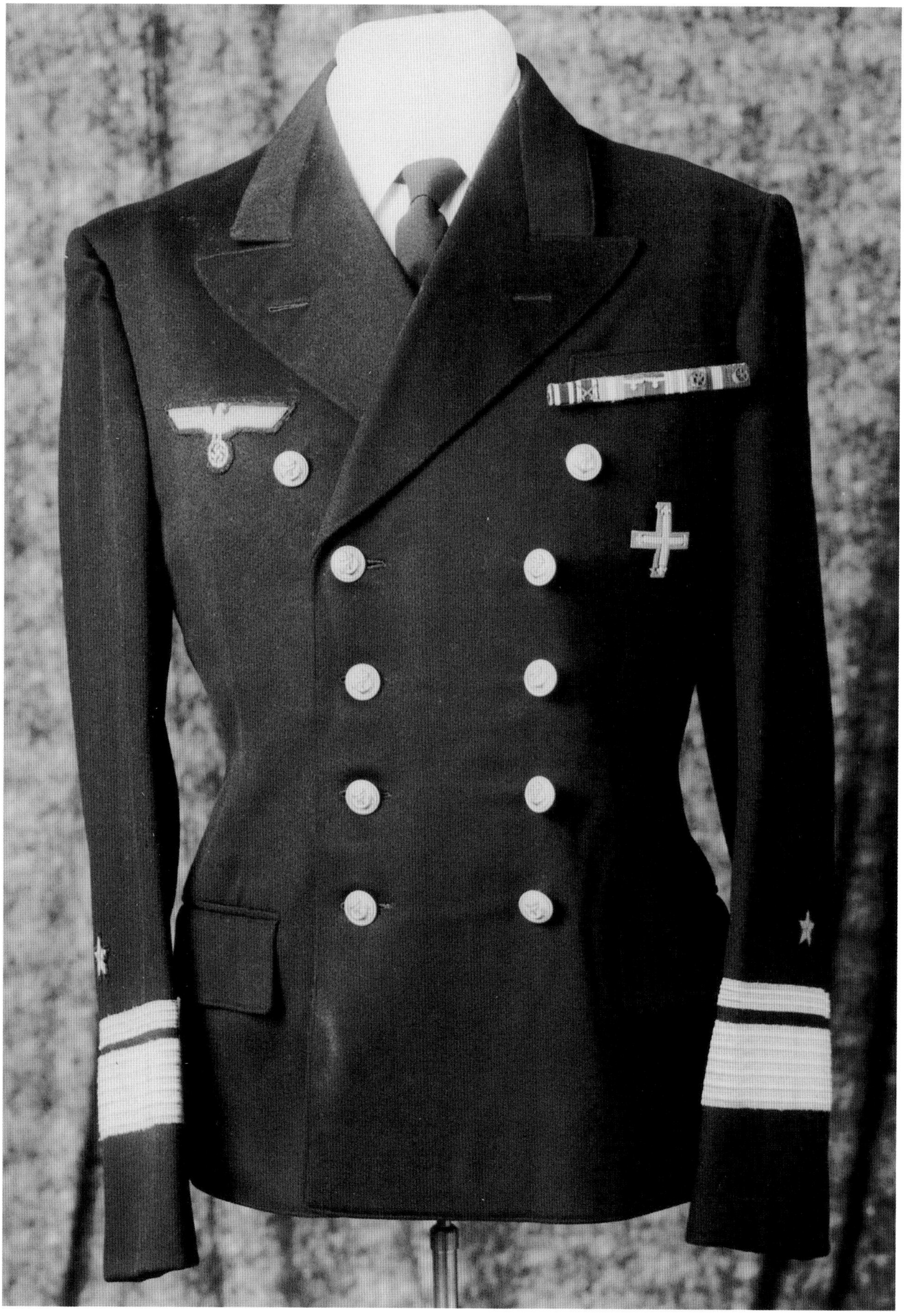

Von Puttkamer's blue reefer jacket. Von Puttkamer was Hitler's naval adjutant and a member of Hitler's so-called "inner circle." *(Moran)*

Von Puttkamer's white summer jacket with hand embroidered gold breast eagle, and removeable Konteradmiral shoulder boards with white underlay.

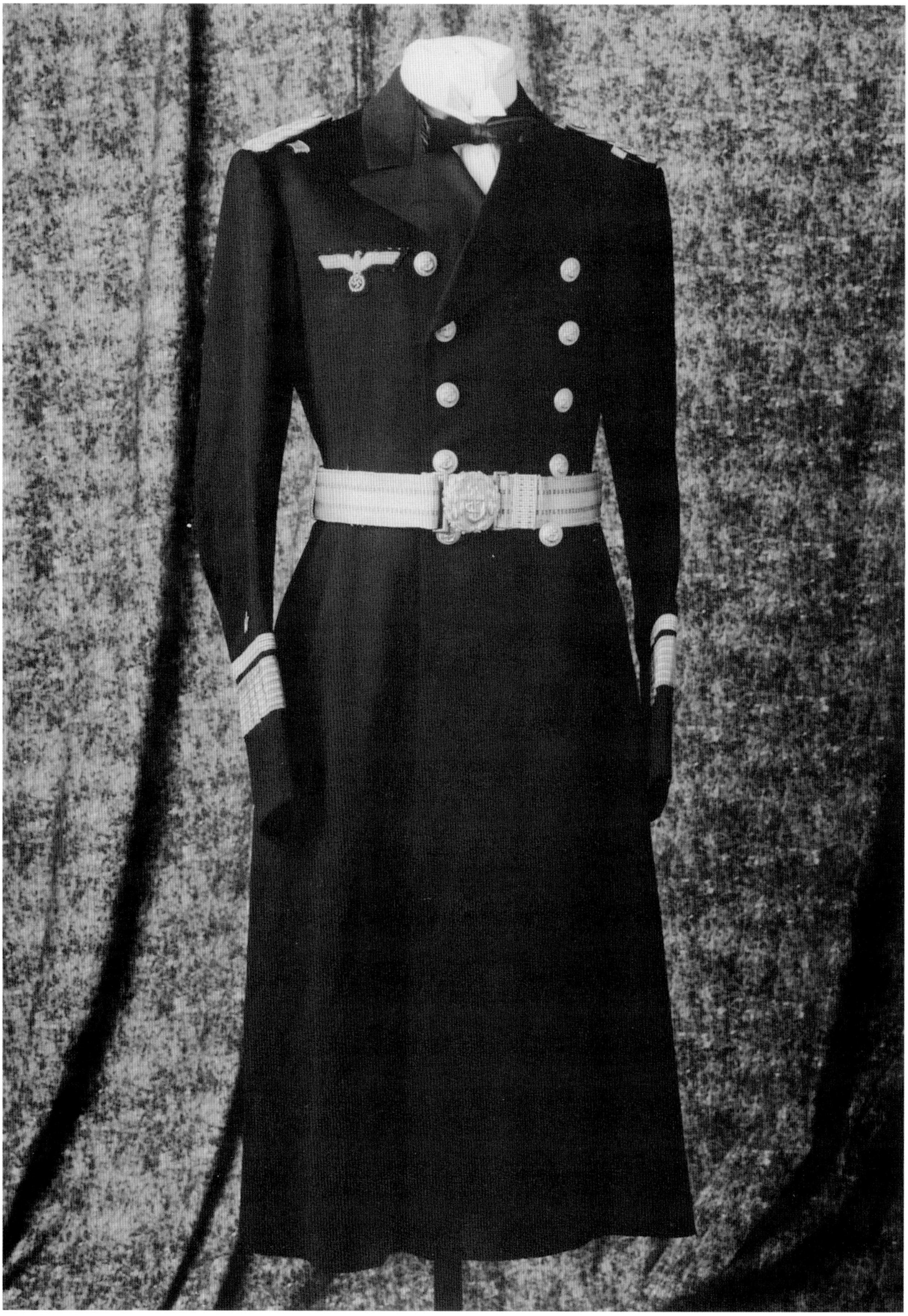

Von Puttkamer's frock coat with Konteradmiral shoulder boards and brocade dress belt. The frock coat was tailored by the firm TH. THOL of Kiel in 1938.

Von Puttkamer's leather greatcoat with Konteradmiral shoulder boards.

Von Puttkamer in leather greatcoat, with the rank of Fregattenkapitän, conversing with Hitler.

Von Puttkamer is seen here greeting Admiral Dönitz. Von Puttkamer was promoted to Konteradmiral on September 1, 1943.

Von Puttkamer wearing his white summer jacket.

The Reefer Jacket of a Kriegsmarine Konteradmiral of Naval Engineers

The coat is displayed with the waist belt and dagger. It is an early war uniform dated 1936.

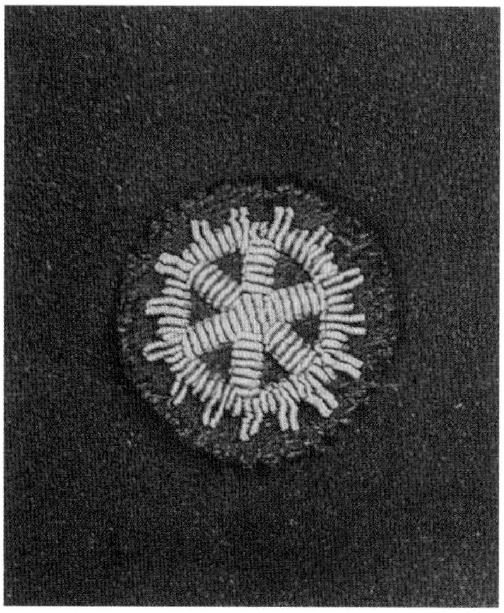

Detail of World War I Iron Cross ribbon in button hole with 1939 Spange for second award.

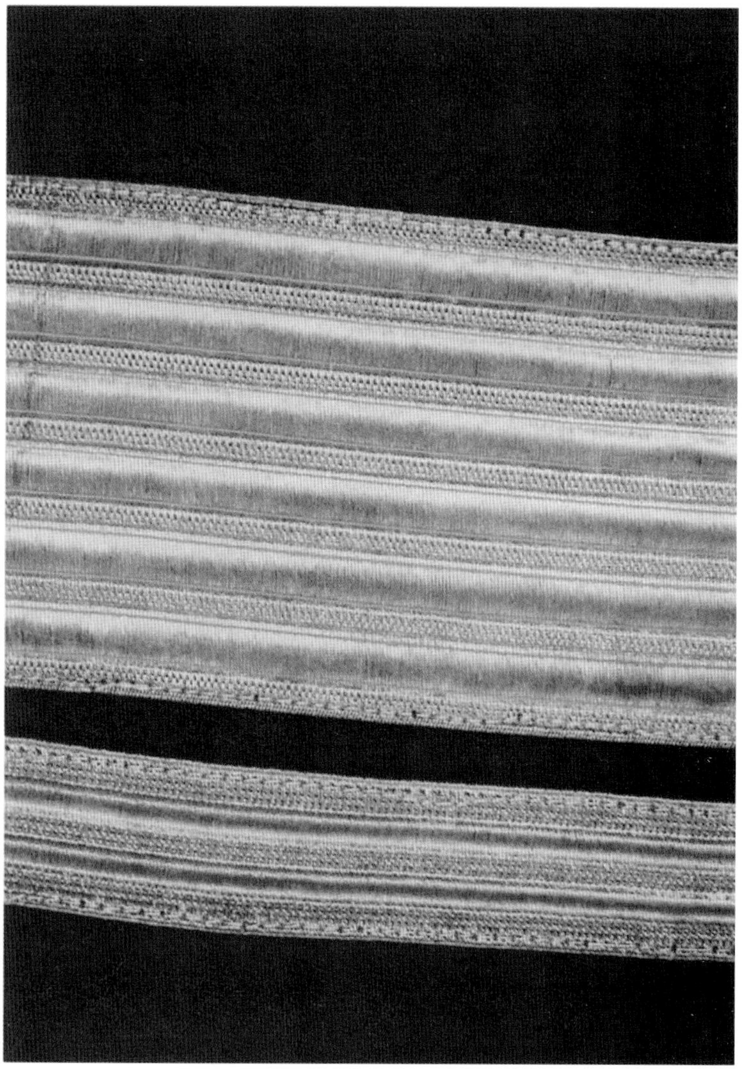

Detail of sleeve braid.

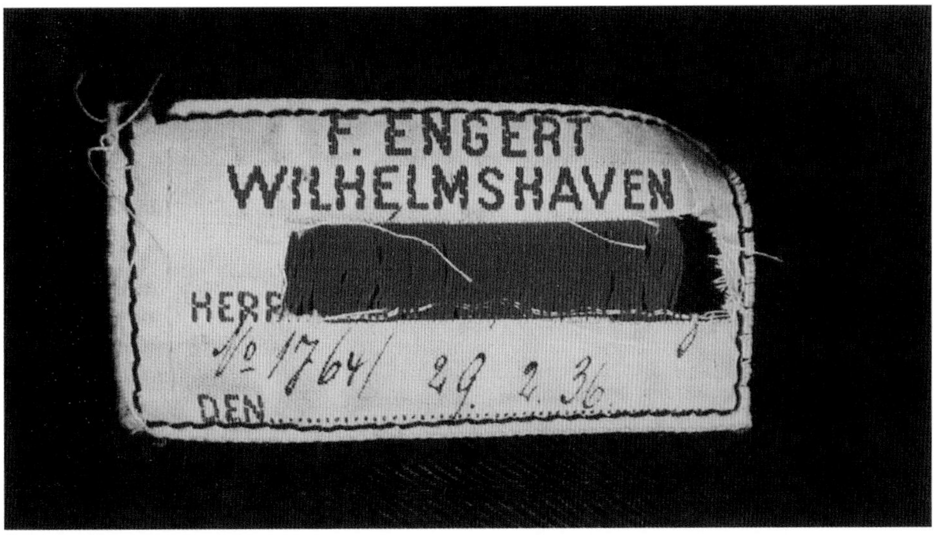

The tailor's label with owners name removed. Note it was made in Wilhelmshaven and is dated 29. 2. 36.

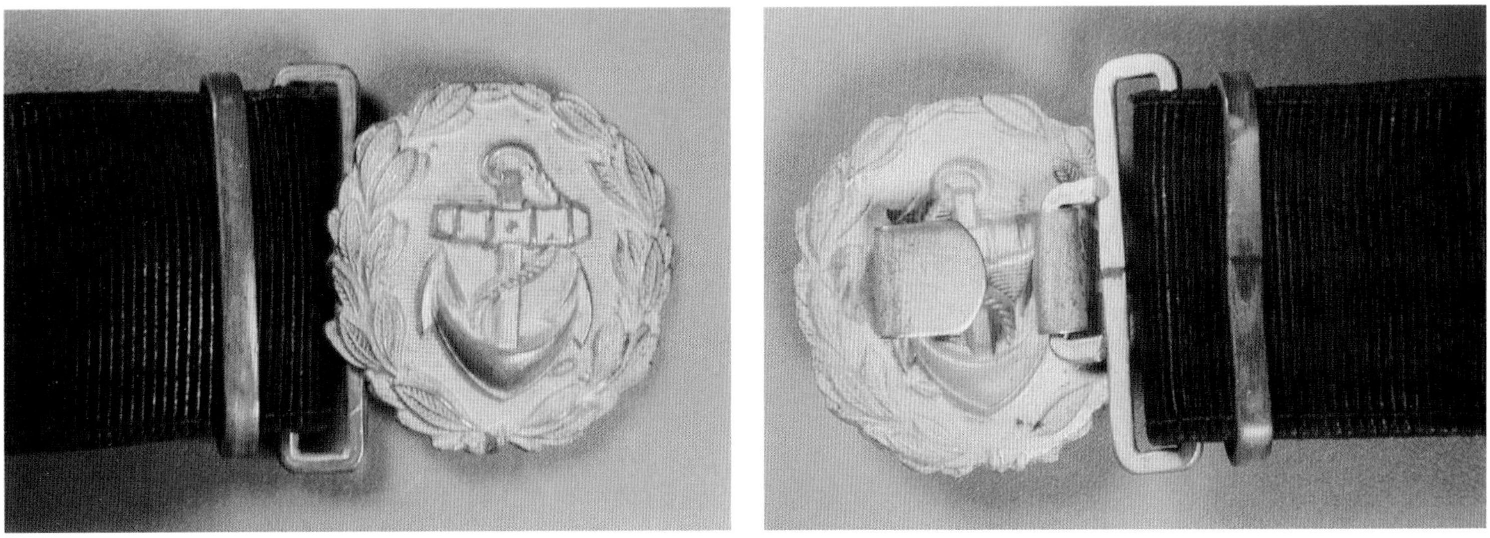

Detail of belt fittings.

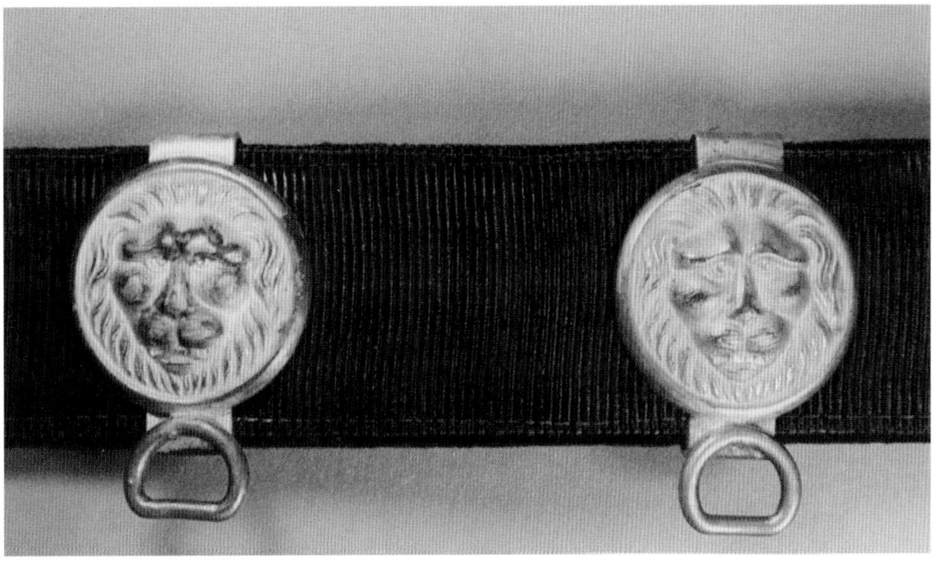

The Reefer Jacket of a Kriegsmarine Administrative Konteradmiral - Verwaltungsbeamte, Hohere Dienst Grad

This jacket has silver bullion trim which indicates that it is administrative. It features a sewn on ribbon bar, and all buttons are marked "Kreigsmarine 42."

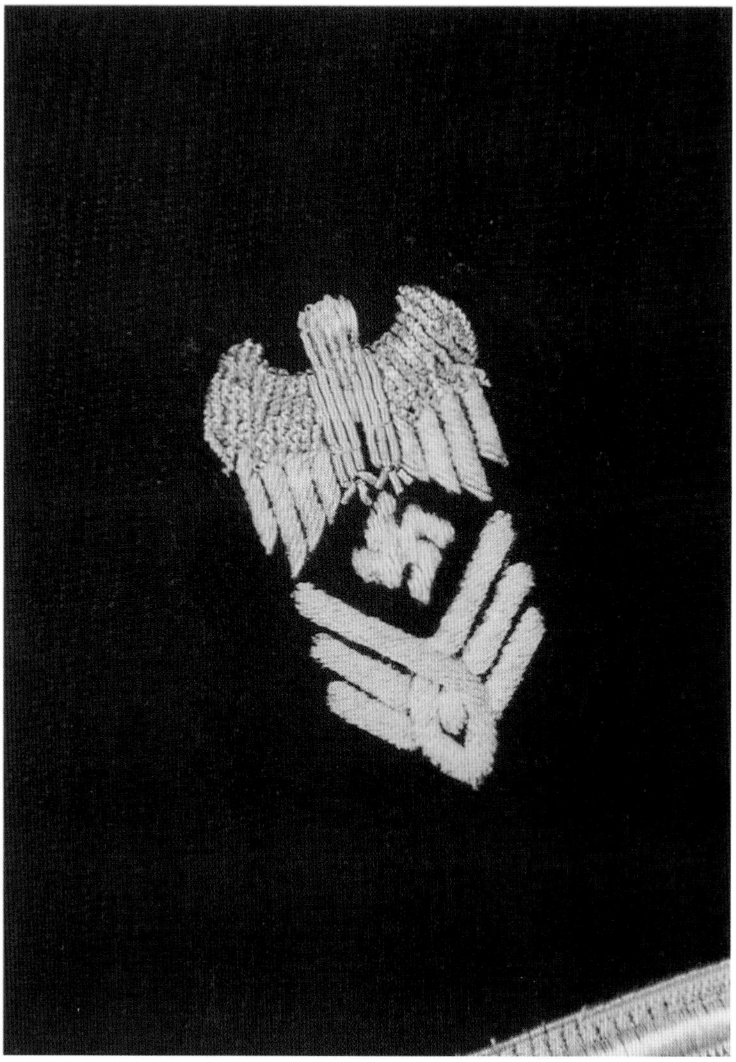

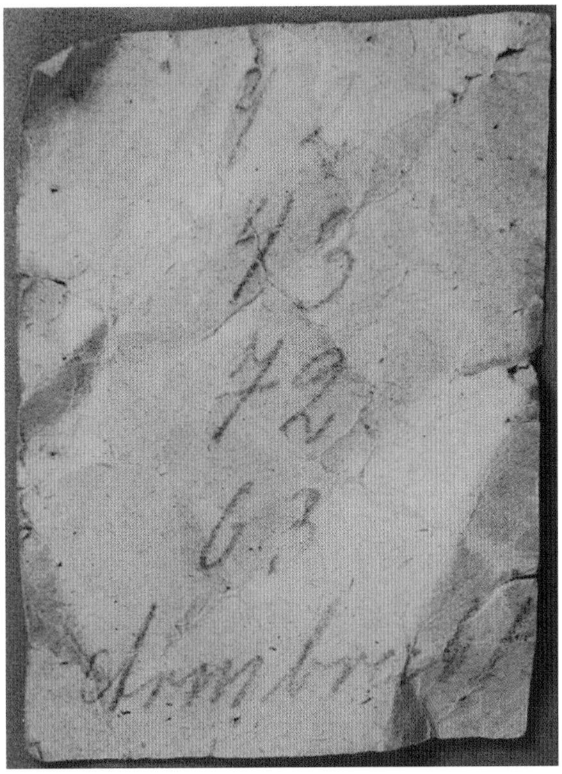

Hand written tailor's measurements with name, found inside of pocket.

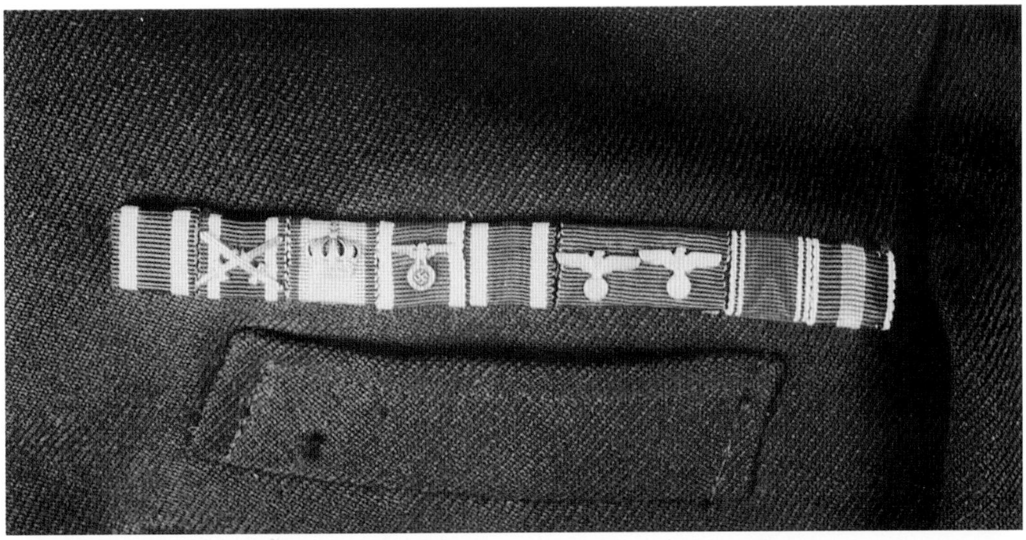

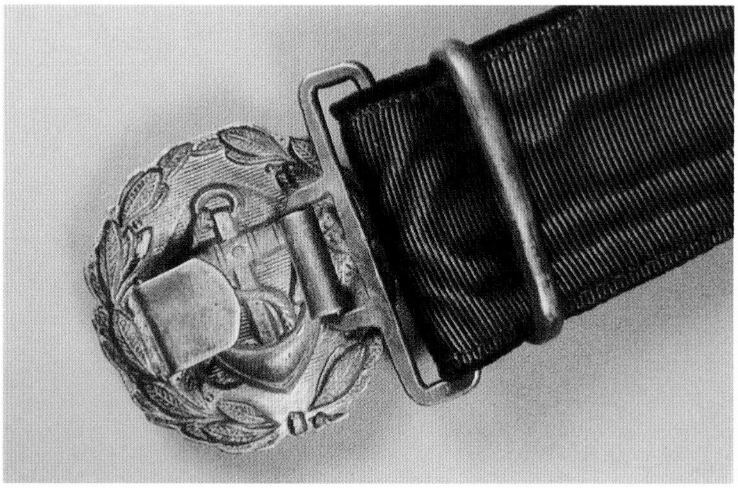

Detail of silver fittings on administrative officer's sword belt.

Detail of silver brocade administrative officer's dress belt and buckle.

The Reefer Jacket of Knight's Cross Holder, Fregattenkapitän Buchting

This uniform is displayed with Knight's Cross, E-Boat Badge, Wound Badge, and Iron Cross.

Fregattenkapitän Buchting in 1943.

Buchting's cap.

Buchting's name sewn in his cap.

The frock coat worn by Buchting. Also pictured is the Kriegsmarine officer's fore-and-aft hat.

An E-Boat at speed.

Elastolin Kriegsmarine toy soldiers.

Kriegsmarine officer's sword. Right: Detail of high quality engraving on sword.

Uniform of Korvettenkapitän Heinrich Bleichrodt

U-boat commander, and Oak Leaves recipient Heinrich Bleichrodt's blue reefer jacket. The jacket was tailored by the firm J. Robrecht of Kiel in 1937. *(Moran)*

Bleichrodt's blue visor cap.

Bleichrodt wearing the blue reefer jacket. Bleichrodt was awarded the Knight's Cross on October 24, 1940 as commander of U-48. He received the Oak Leaves on September 23, 1942 while in command of U-109.

Uniform of Kapitän zur See Hans Rehm

Knight's Cross recipient Kapitän zur See Hans Rehm's blue reefer jacket. The jacket was tailored by the firm Thorn of Paris in 1941. *(Moran)*

Rehm's blue visor cap. Cap has removable blue top with a white satin lining.

Left: Rehm was awarded the Knight's Cross on December 31, 1941 as a Korvettenkapitän and Chief Minesweeper 2. Flotille. Right: Rehm wearing his blue reefer jacket.

The Reefer Jacket of Kriegsmarine Administrative Oberleutnant

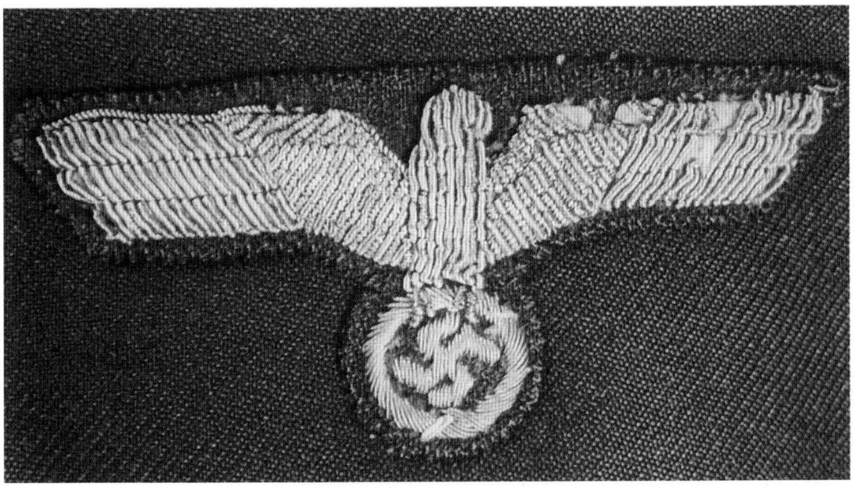

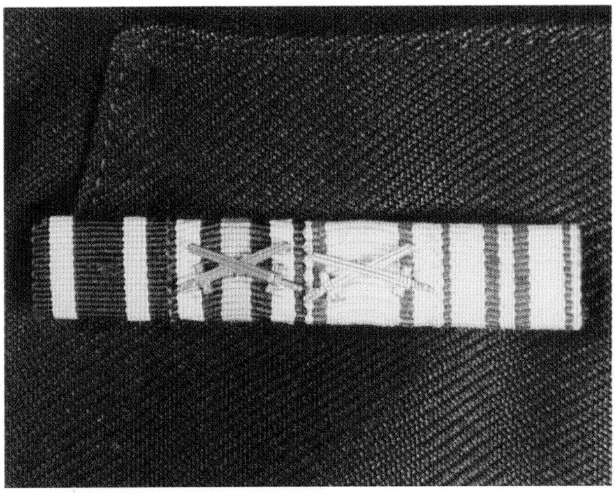

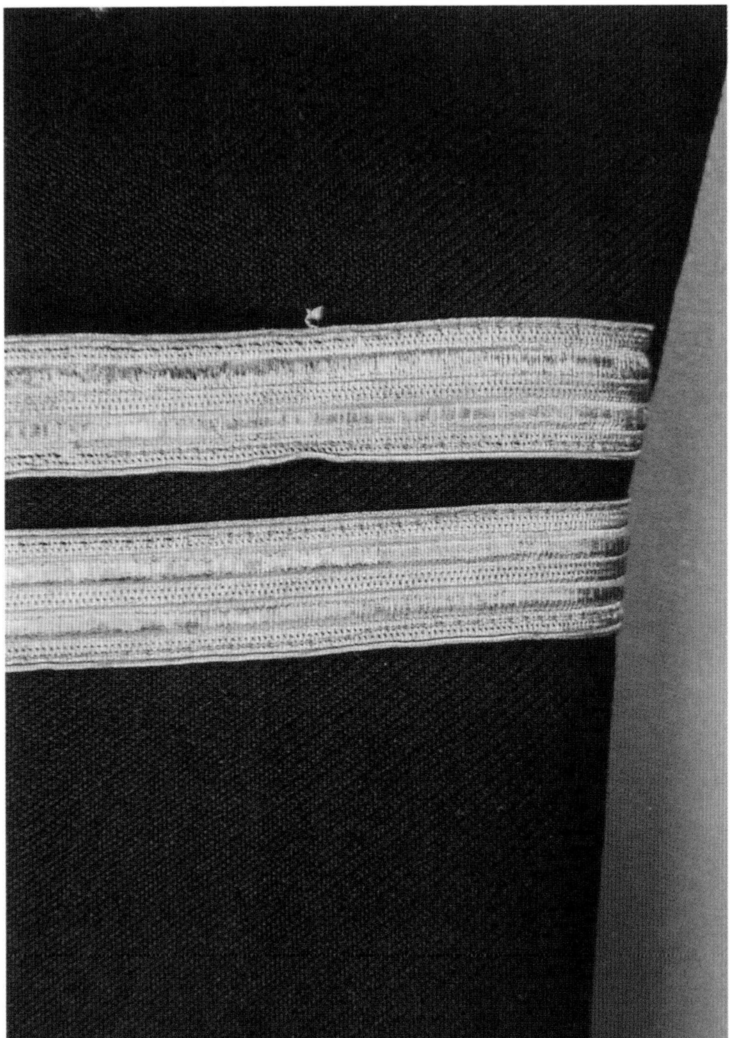

Kriegsmarine administrative officer's visor cap.

4

SS and Police

The Uniform of an Allgemeine-SS Oberführer

This coat has the first type rank insignia worn from August of 1929 to April of 1942. The sleeve title is for SS Sub-district XXX. The Old Fighter's Chevron is on the right sleeve and the SS Kampfbinde (brassard) is on the left sleeve. The tunic is displayed with the brocade dress belt.

XXX

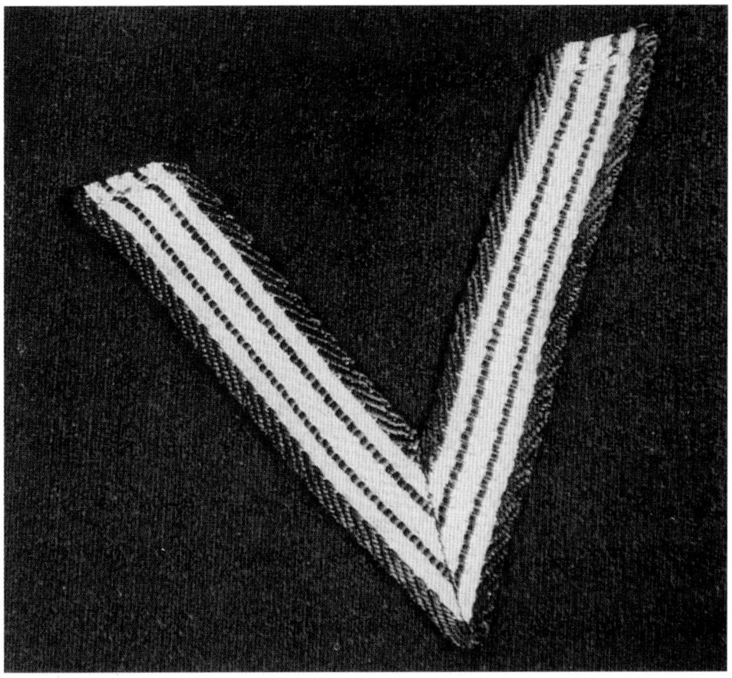

Detail of brocade dress belt and buckle.

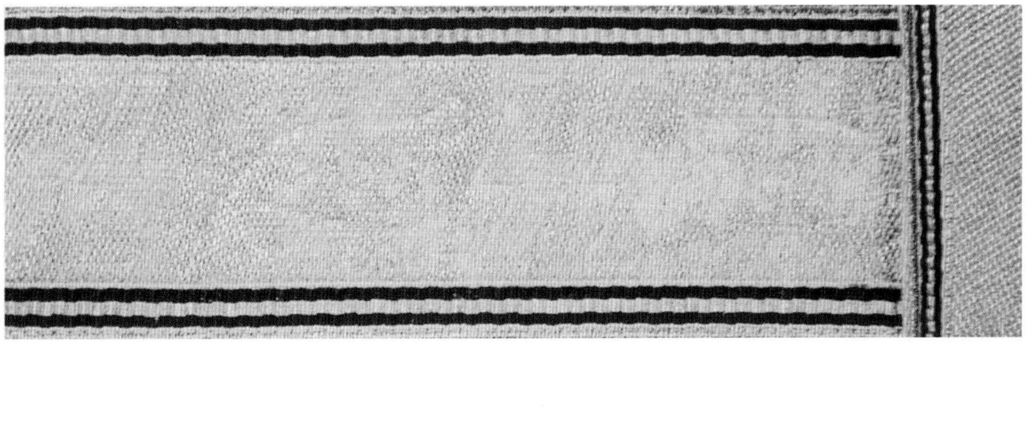

Allgemeine-SS General officer's visor cap.

The Black Service Tunic of an Allgemeine-SS Obersturmführer of the "Thuringen" Standarte

This coat is displayed with the leather officer's belt and cross strap.

Thüringen

Thüringen

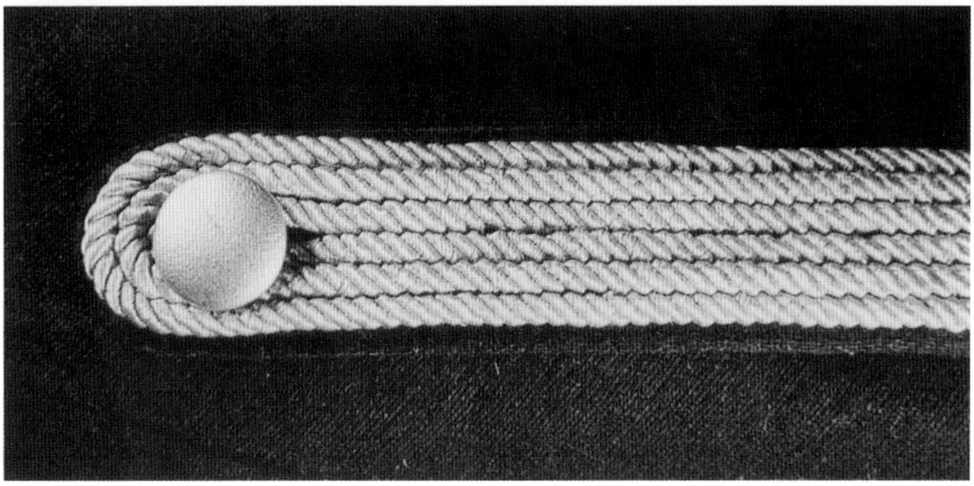

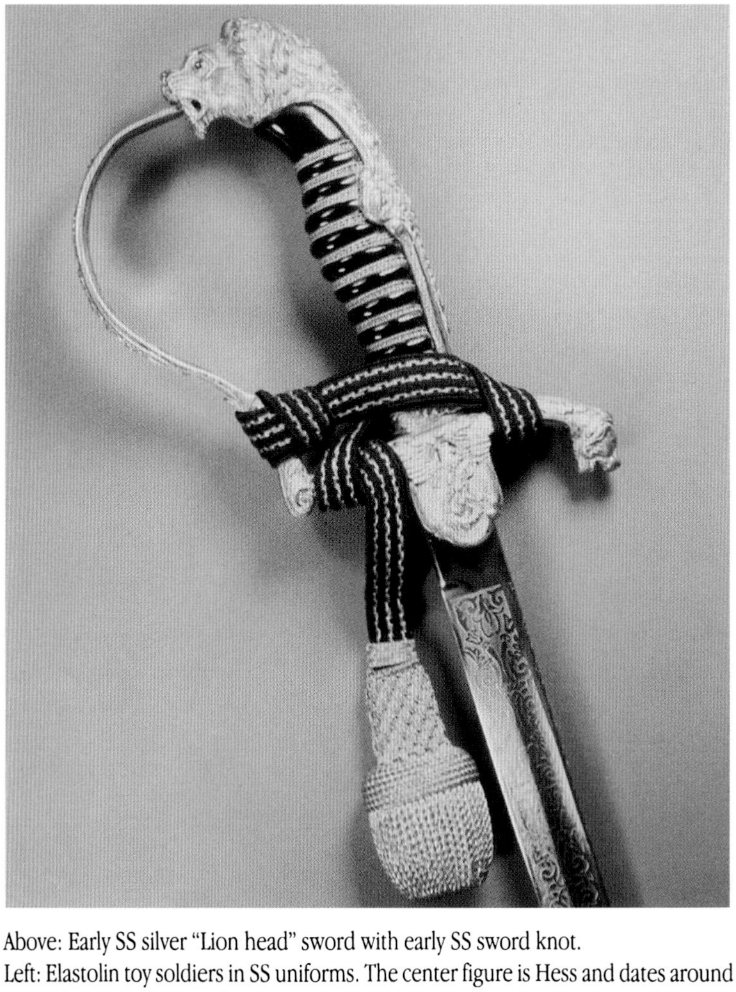

Above: Early SS silver "Lion head" sword with early SS sword knot.
Left: Elastolin toy soldiers in SS uniforms. The center figure is Hess and dates around 1936-39. The first figure dates to 1939-40, and the third, to 1935.

Allgemeine-SS officer's visor cap.

White Summer Tunic of an Allgemeine-SS Untersturmführer

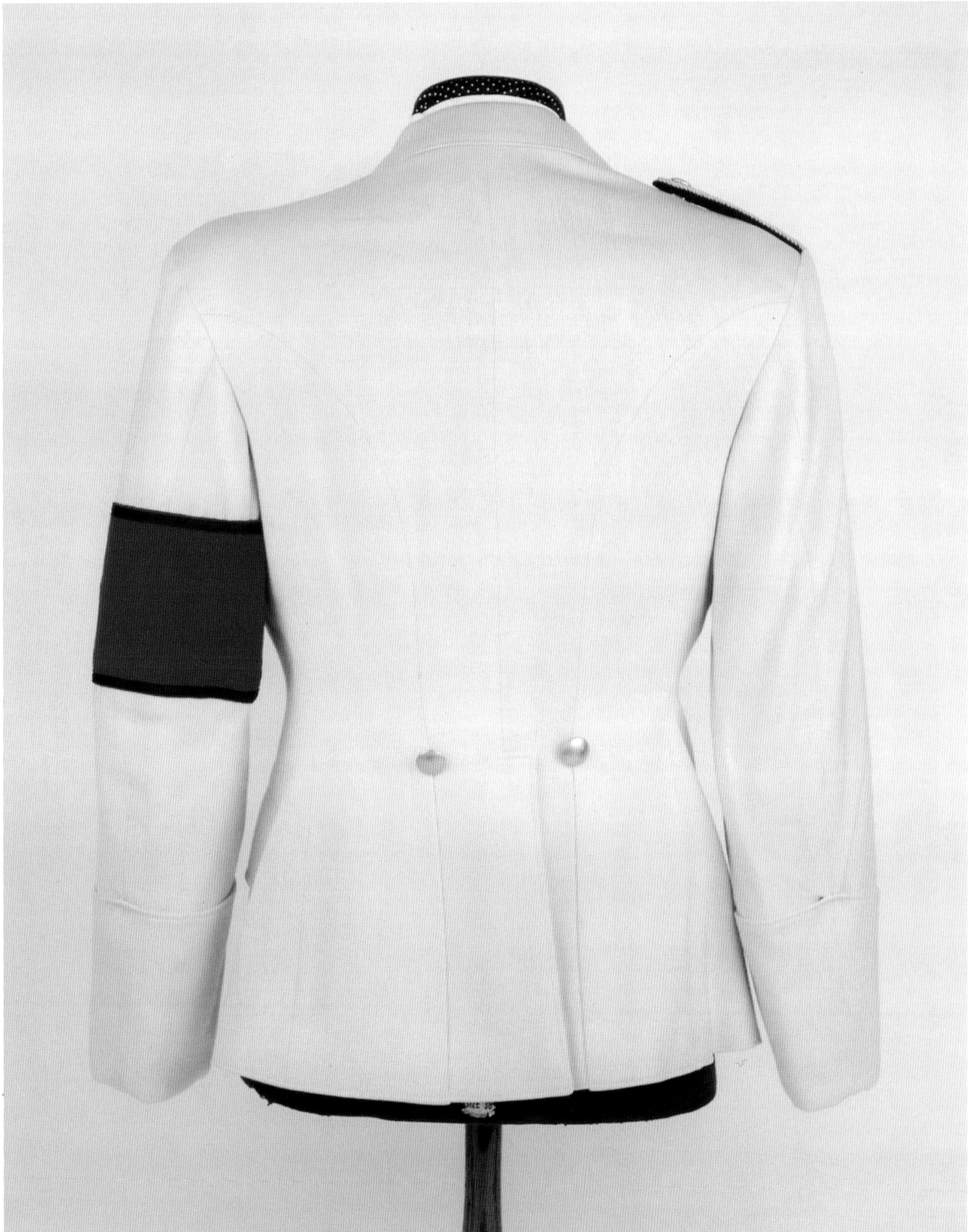

MASSCHNEIDEREI
ANDR. STÖCKL
NÜRNBERG

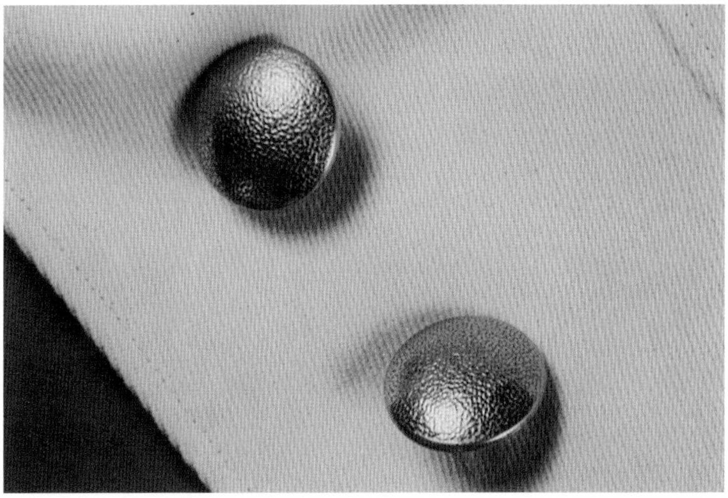

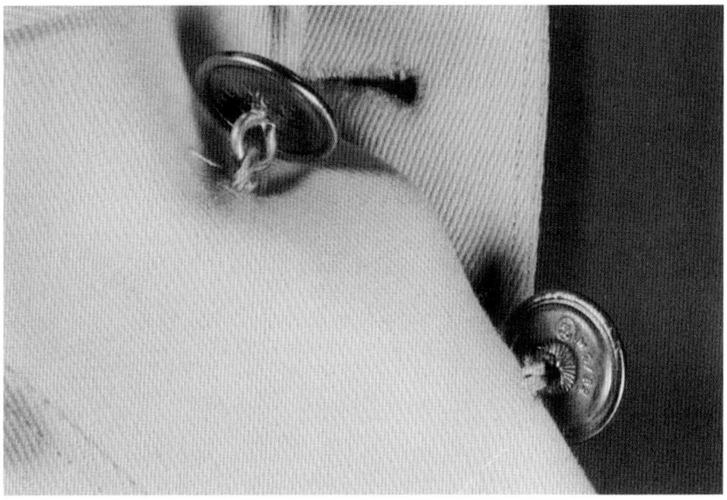

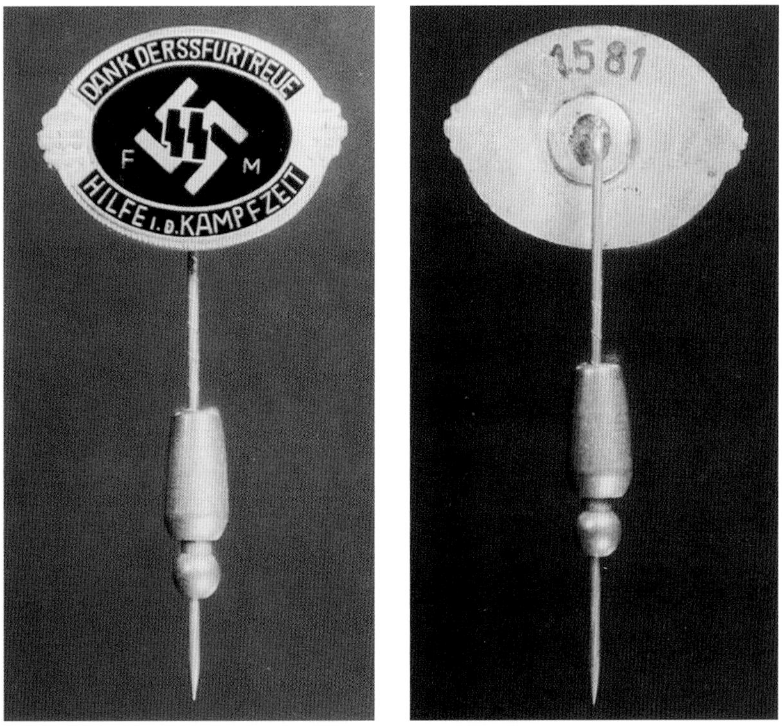

Stick pin given for financial donations to the SS.

Black Service Dress Tunic of an SS Scharführer of the "Germania" Standarte

This coat is displayed with the standard proofed leather belt and cross strap.

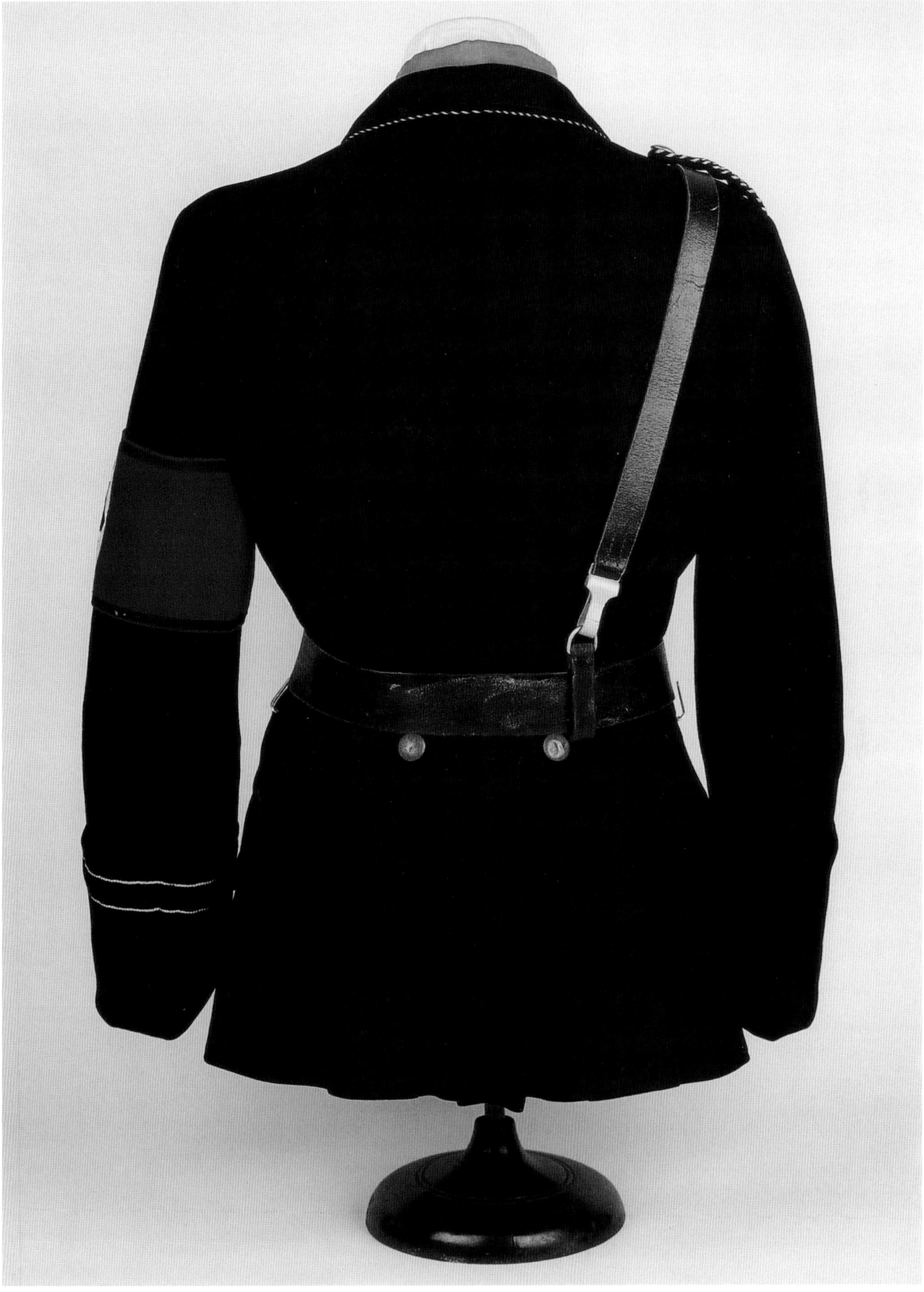

Germania

2

Germania

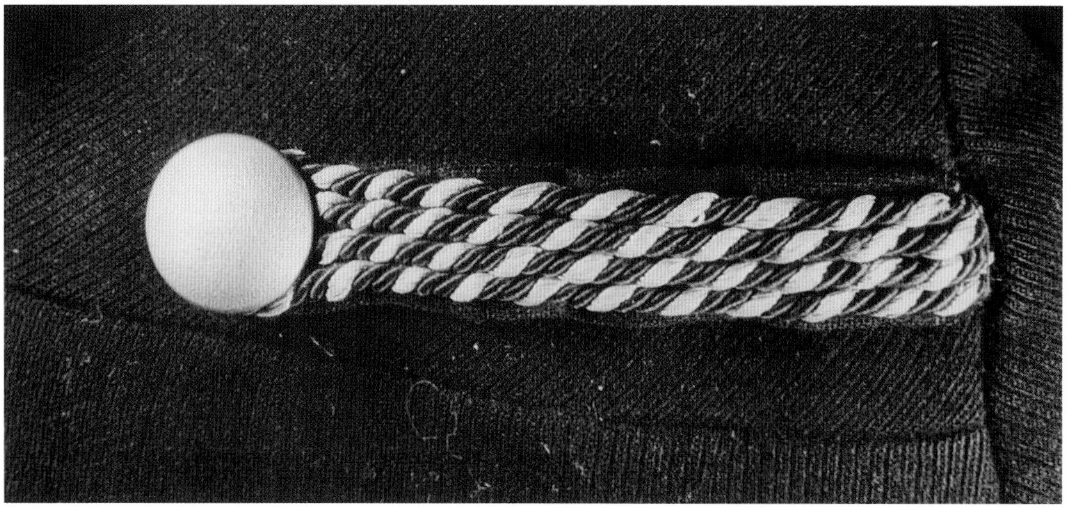

Detail of Belt buckle and fittings.

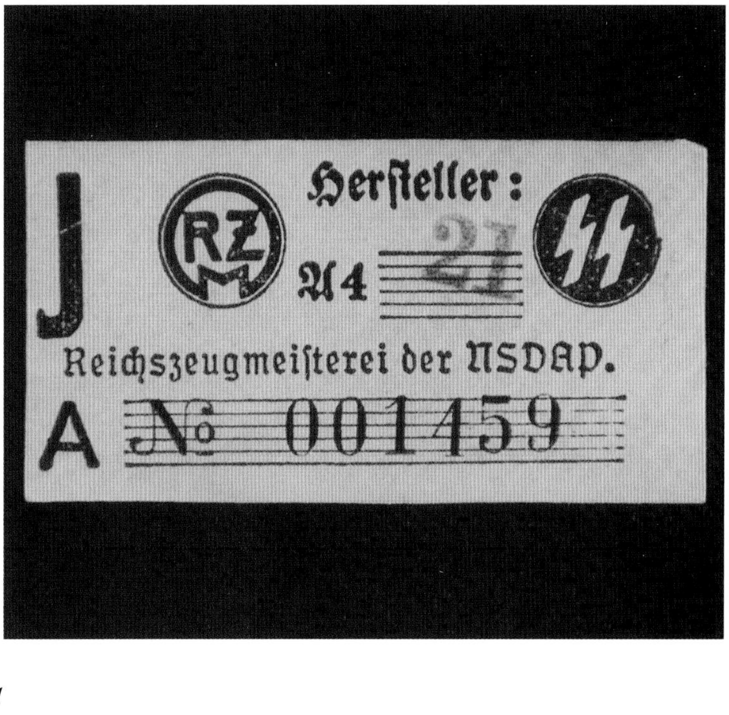

Right: Detail of an SS proof tag as used on several cloth items.

SS trooper wearing the early style helmet of the Deutschland Division.

Left: SS men guarding the Austrian Crown jewels.

Early photo of a mounted SS trooper.

Enlisted Man's Italian 29th Waffen-SS Grenadier Division Tunic

This tunic has private purchase SS style sleeve insignia which is possibly hand embroidered or single run machine embroidered. Collar tabs are also private purchase. *(Matthew Reinert, MHS)*

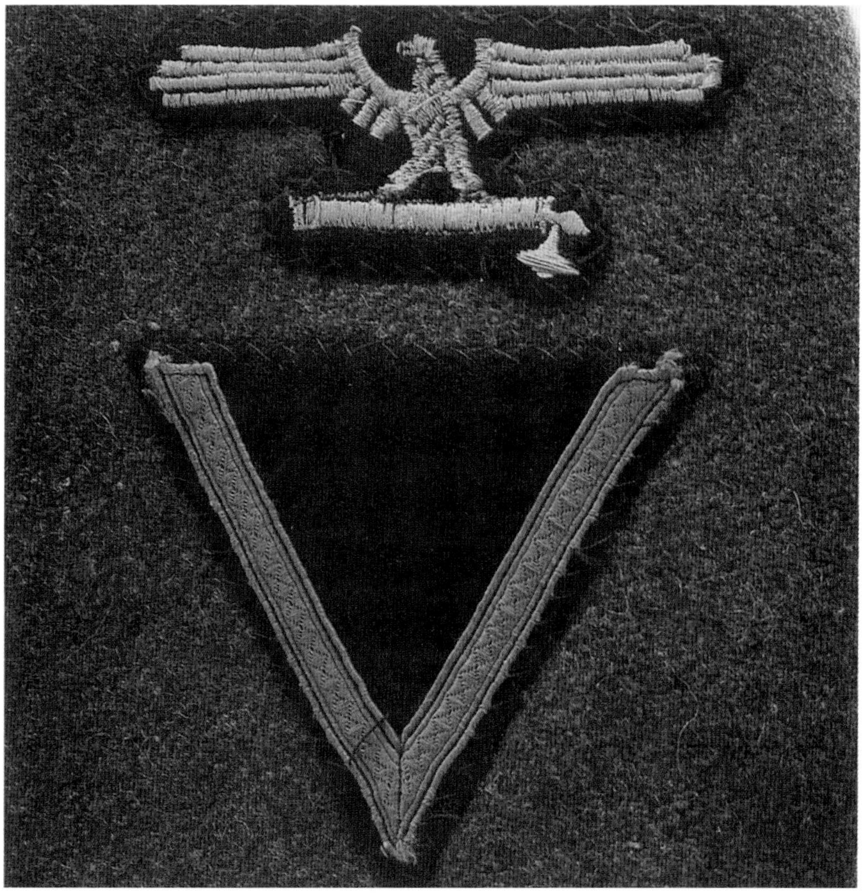

Enlisted 13th Waffen-SS Handschar Division Denim (Reed Green) Tunic

This tunic has regulation collar tabs, eagle on left sleeve, and "edelweiss" mountain unit insignia on right sleeve. Note loops on left front pocket are heavily stitched and oval outline may indicate that the Anti-partisan Badge was worn. Note also the short cut lower pockets. *(Matthew Reinert, MHS)*

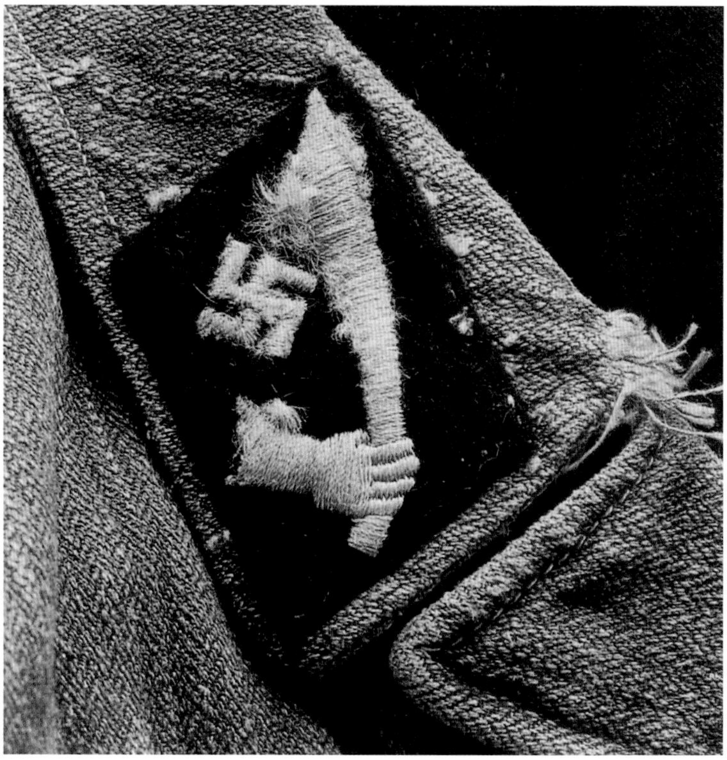

Enlisted 13th Waffen-SS Handschar Division Tunic

This tunic is made of course wool and is an unusually large size. The breast pockets were removed (which was common practice in the unit) loops for medals were added. The tunic features standard mountain piped shoulder boards and standard machine embroidered Croatian checkerboard insignia on left sleeve. The NCO quality sleeve eagle appears to be sewn over an earlier sleeve eagle. Note the early hand embroidered collar tabs. *(Matthew Reinert, MHS)*

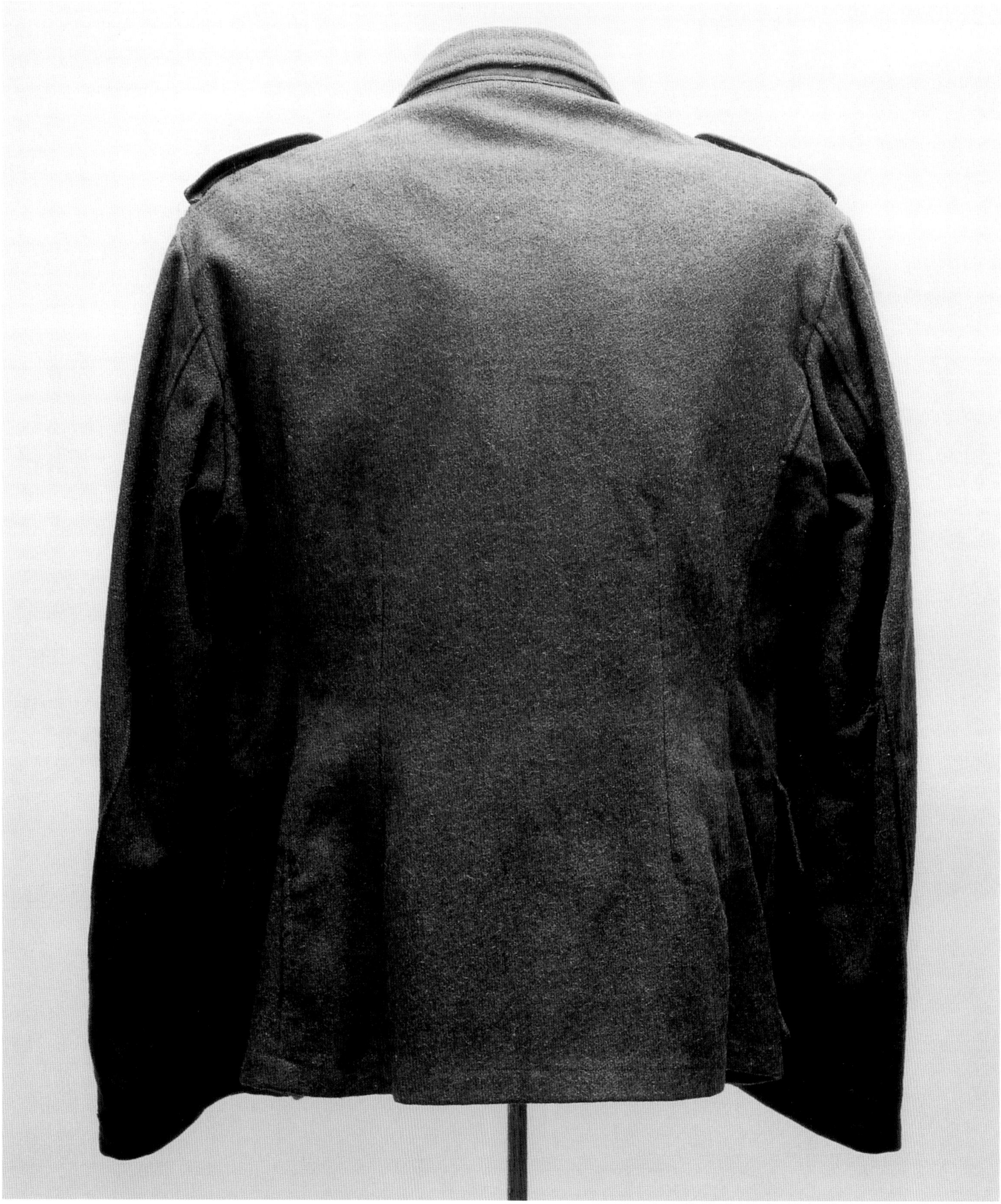

Early NCO Italian SS Tunic

This tunic features the early distinctive red background insignia. Note the right collar tab is blank and shoulder boards are private purchase. *(Matthew Reinert, MHS)*

Early Waffen-SS Denim (Reed Green) Tunic with Pleated Pockets

This tunic is constructed of heavy material and has early machine embroidered collar tabs and sleeve eagle. The insignia is tightly sewn in place. Shoulder boards are piped in pink for Panzer troops. *(Matthew Reinert, MHS)*

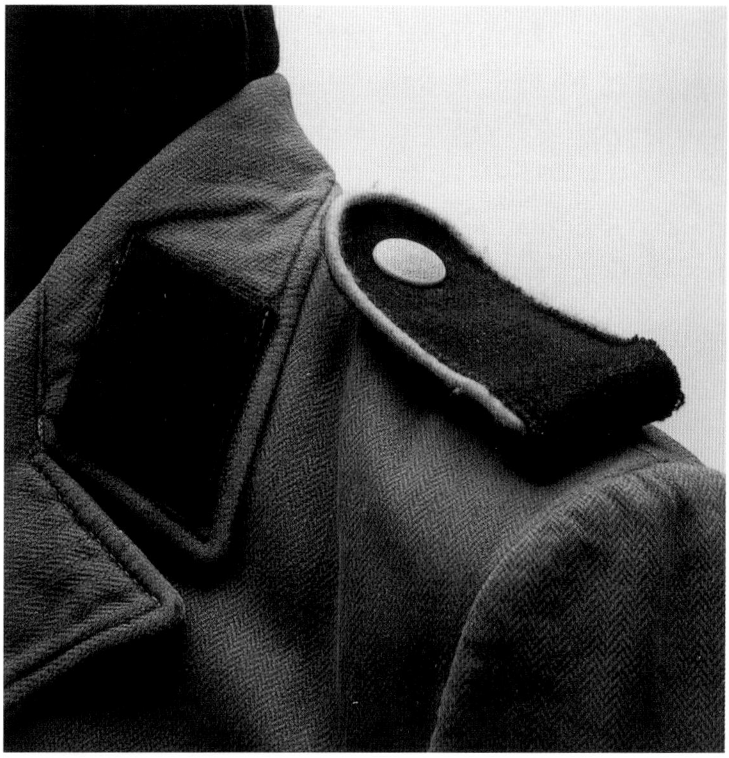

Waffen-SS Officer's Overcoat

This coat was worn by an SS Untersturmführer of the 20th Waffen-Grenadier Division der SS (Estonian volunteers). *(Shea)*

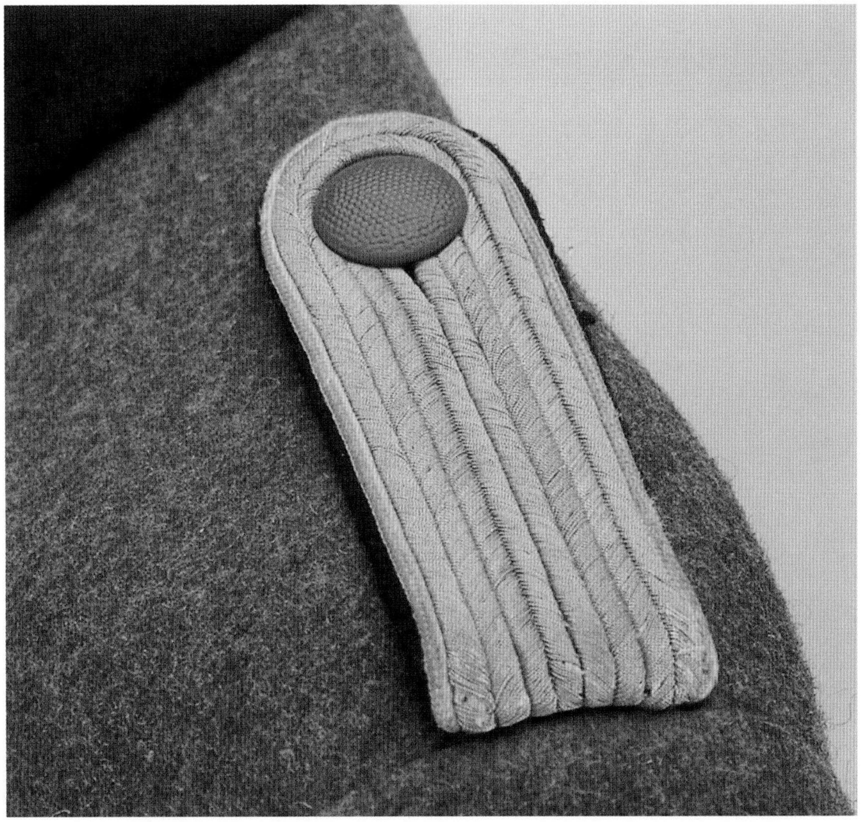

The Tunic of an SS-Police Untersturmführer

This tunic has a silver bullion hand embroidered sleeve insignia and SS-Runes on the lower left pocket. It is a very high quality garment.

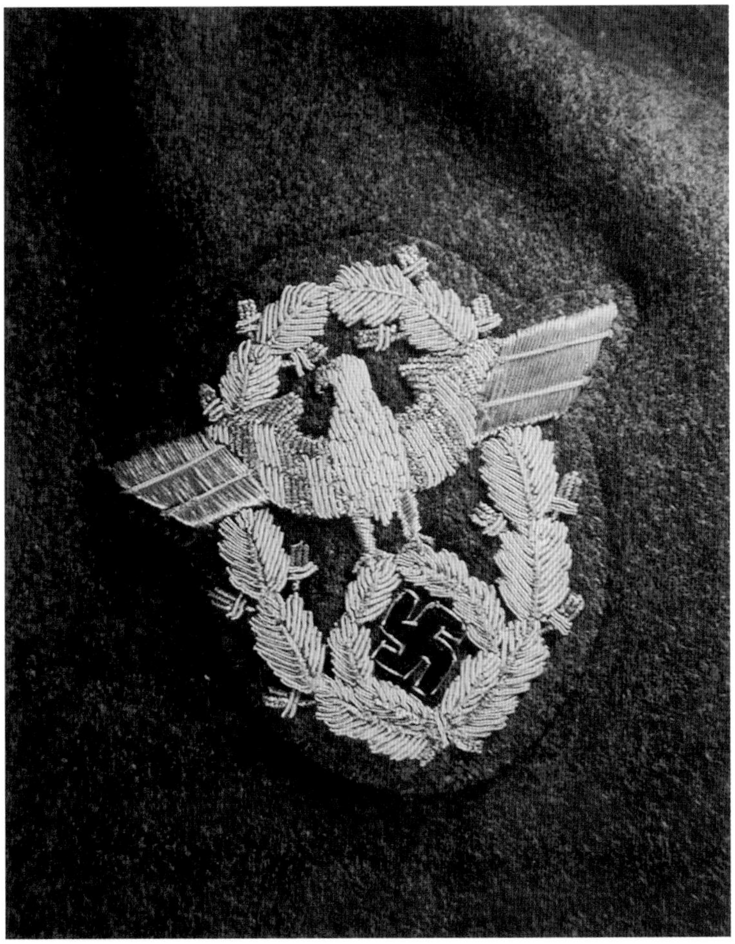

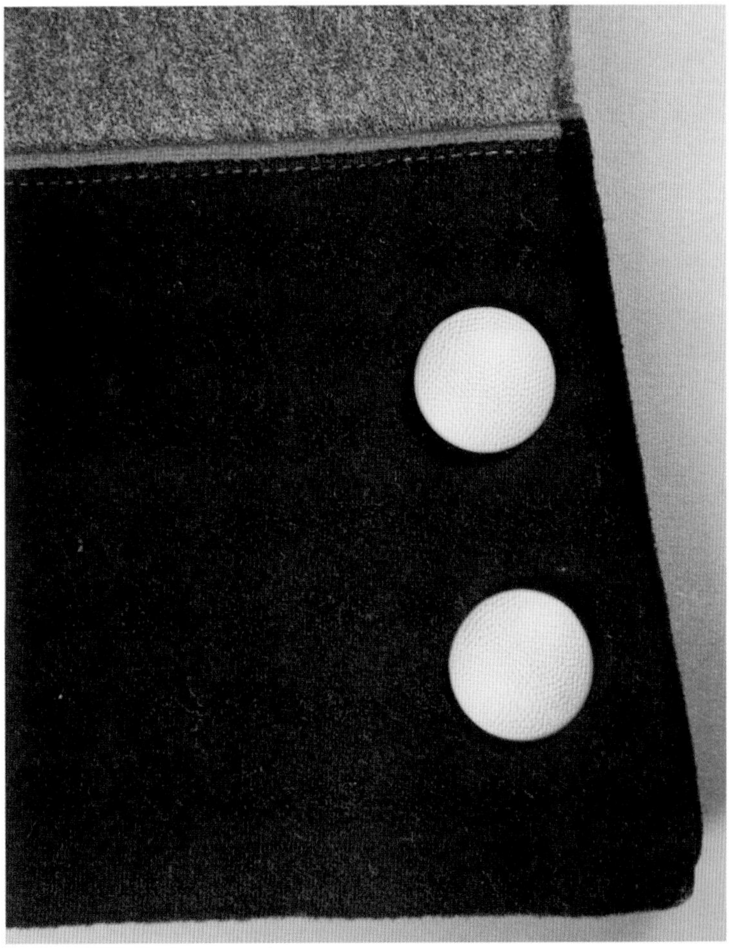

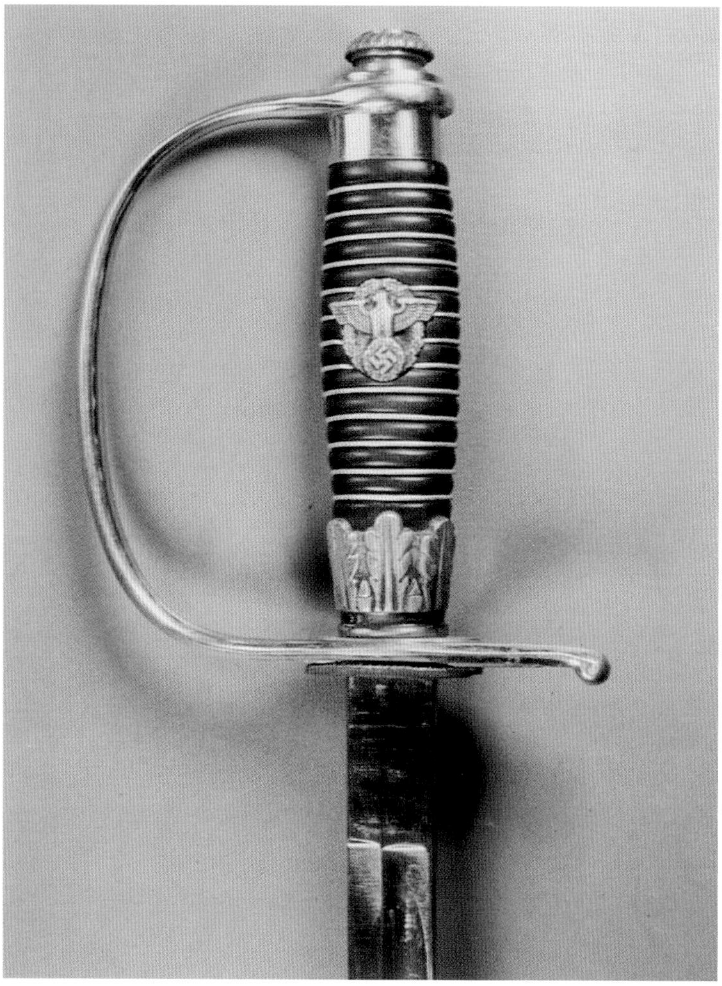

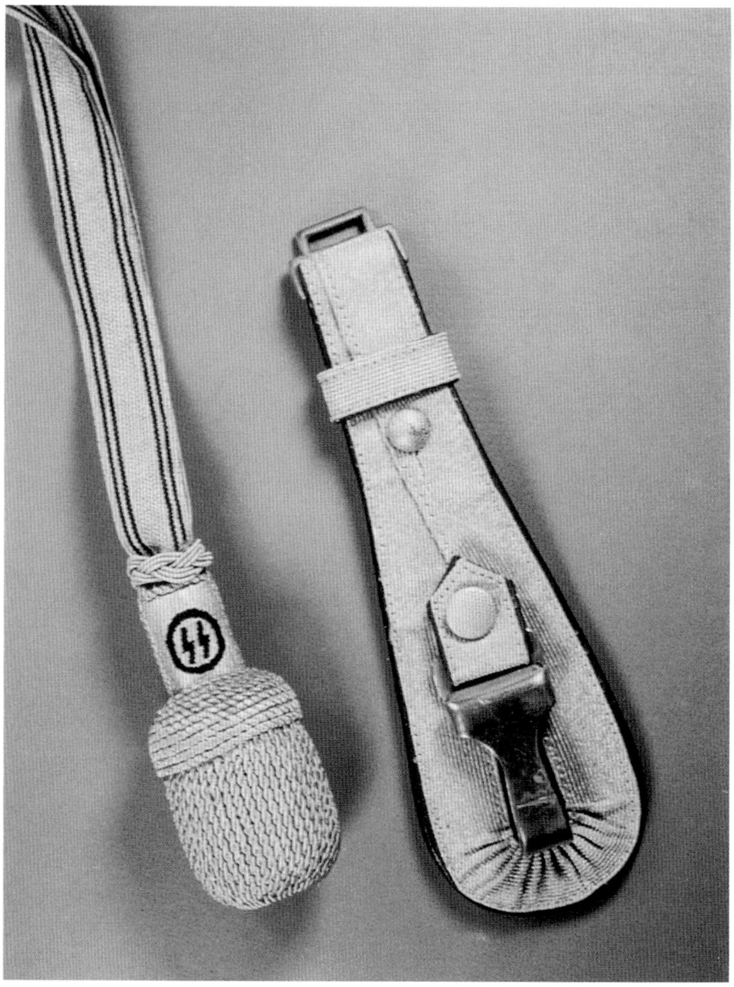

SS-Police Officer's Sword. Right: Sword knot and hanger for Waffen-SS or SS-Police sword.

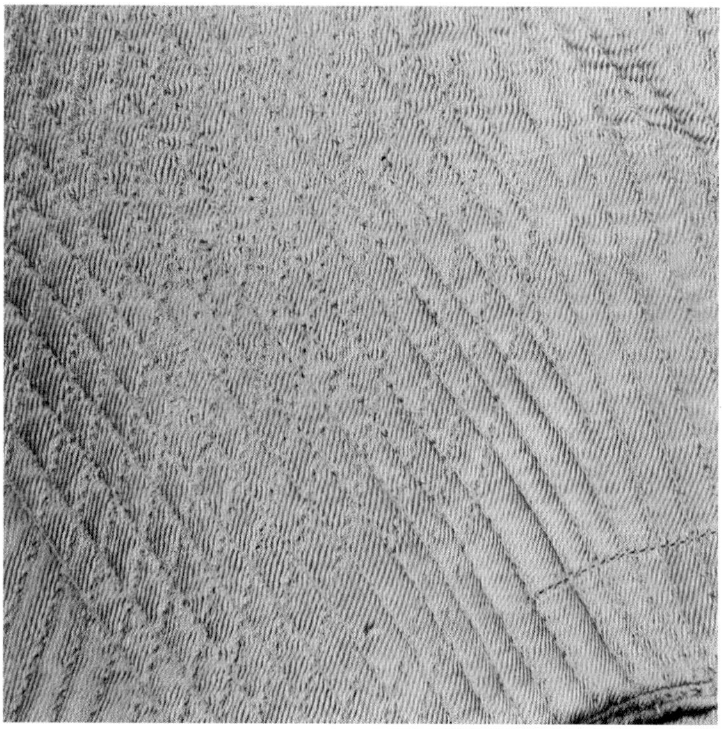

Detail of quilting of interior lining.

Elastolin mounted policeman toy soldier.

5

Political and HJ

Brown Shirt of Reichskanzler Adolf Hitler

This brown shirt was manufactured by the firm of Wilhem Holters, Berlin and is dated July 1935. Two uniques features of the shirt are the tie release strap under the collar, and the cloth loop on the right shoulder for holding the cross strap in place. It was liberated along with other personal items from Hitler's Munich apartment in May of 1945 by 1stLt. Philip Ben Lieber. *(Shea)*

1stLt. Lieber shown with personal effects taken from Hitler's Munich apartment.

NSDAP Political Leaders Tunic

This tunic is for a Stellenleiter in the Gauleitung. It is displayed with the gold brocade belt and gold political aiguillete.

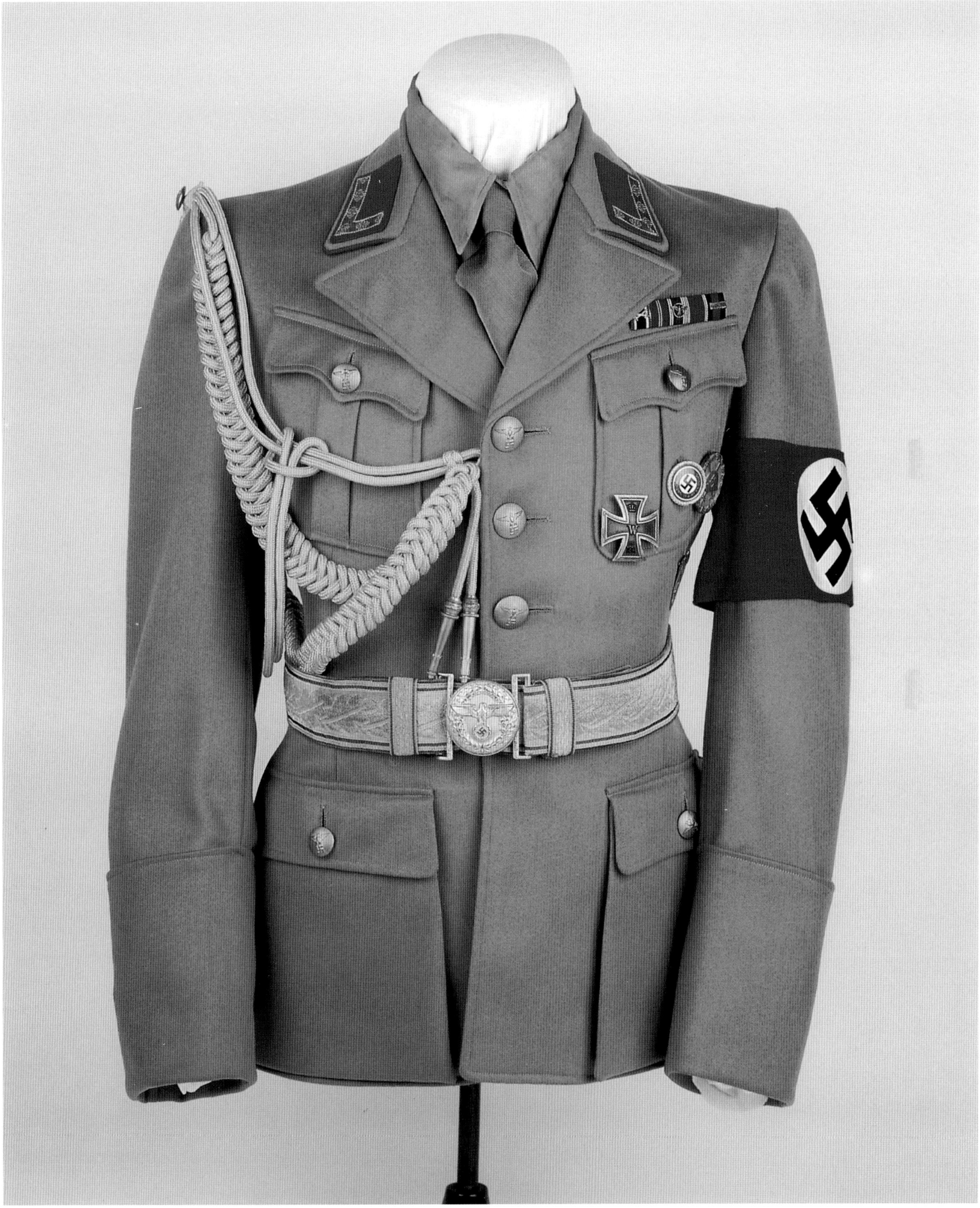

Right: This man is wearing the brown political leader's uniform. His white uniform is the example pictured later in this work.

Political leader's visor cap.

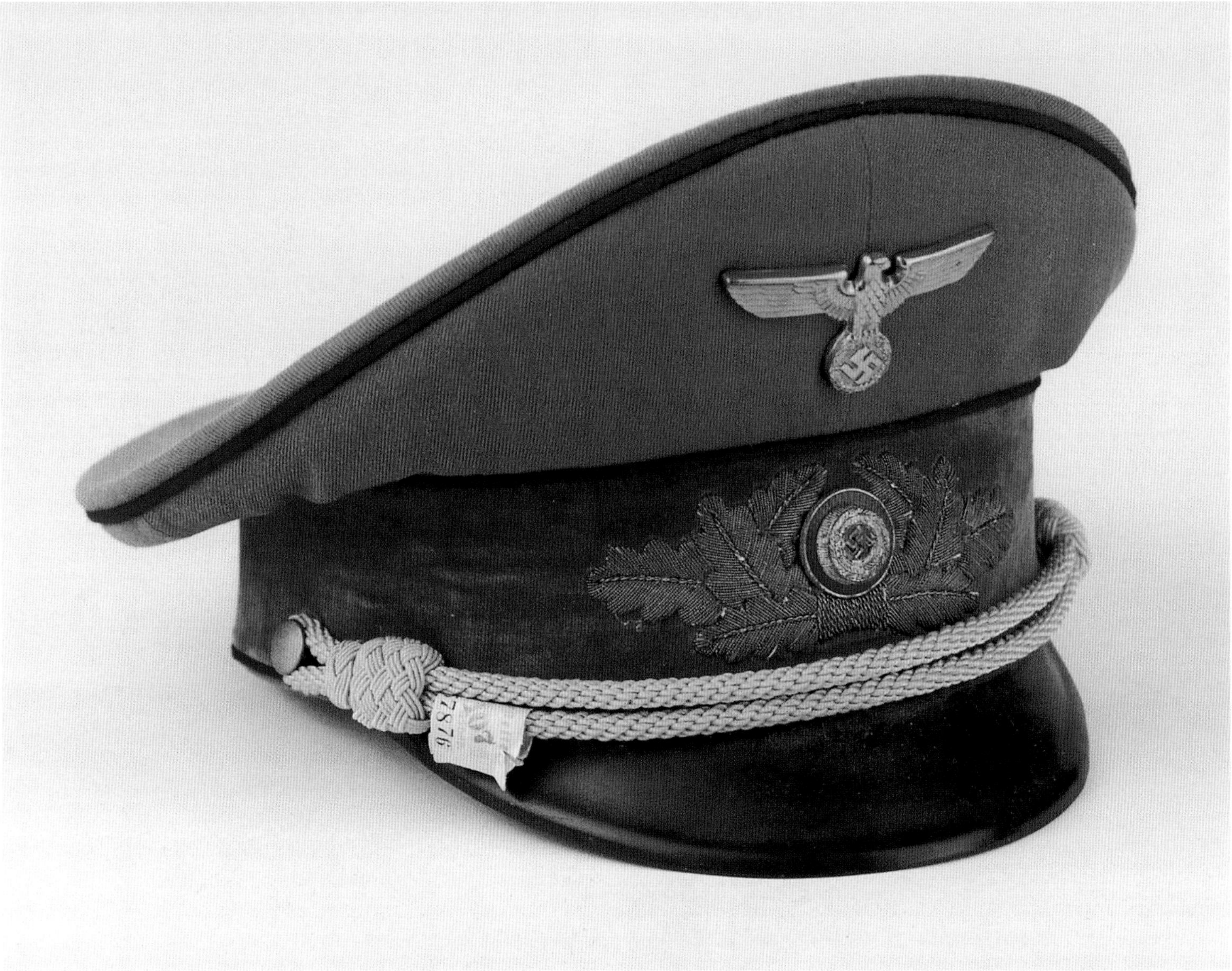

NSDAP Political Leaders Walking Out Dress Uniform for Gau Level

The uniform is red piped for Gau level, collar tabs are for Hauptstellenleiter (main deptartment leader), third pattern 1936-1938. Uniform was worn by Karl Gattringer who is also shown, with his bride, wearing this uniform. His personal identification papers are also shown. *(Shea)*

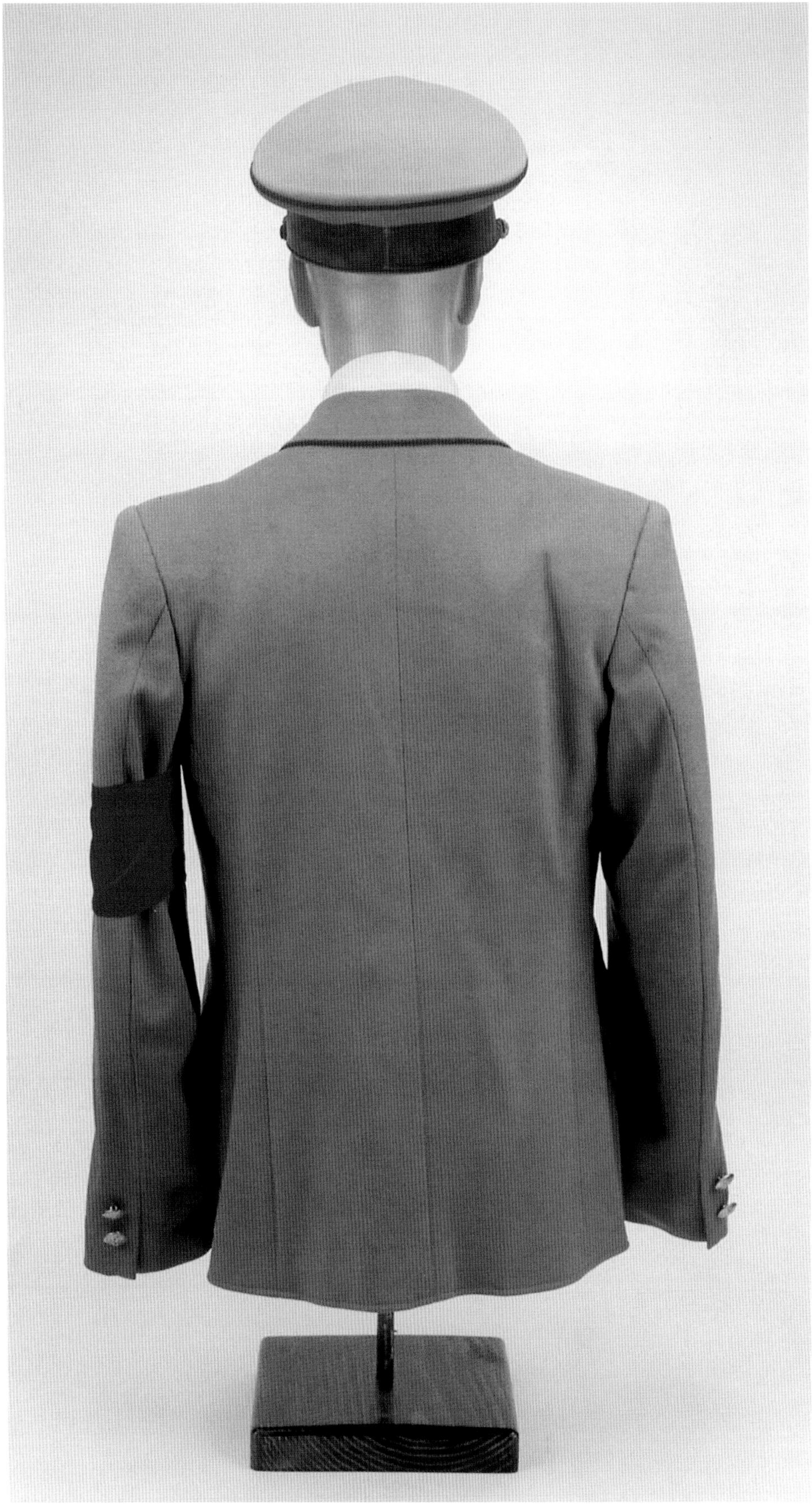

Herr Karl Gattinger
~~Frau~~
~~Fräulein~~
erhält die Erlaubnis, nach Ablegung der Prüfung*) ein Kraftfahrzeug mit Antrieb durch

Verbrennungsmaschine

der Klasse -4- zu führen.

Ried i. I., den 23ten Dez. 1938

Für den Landrat:

(Verwaltungsbehörde.)

(Unterschrift.)

Liste Nr. 2/G

Nach bestandener Prüfung ausgehändigt.

, den 19

Der amtlich anerkannte Sachverständige

(Unterschrift.)

Liste Nr.

*) Bei Führerscheinen der Klasse 4 sind die Worte „nach Ablegung der Prüfung" und der Vermerk über die Aushändigung durch den Sachverständigen zu streichen.

Eigenhändige Unterschrift des Inhabers:

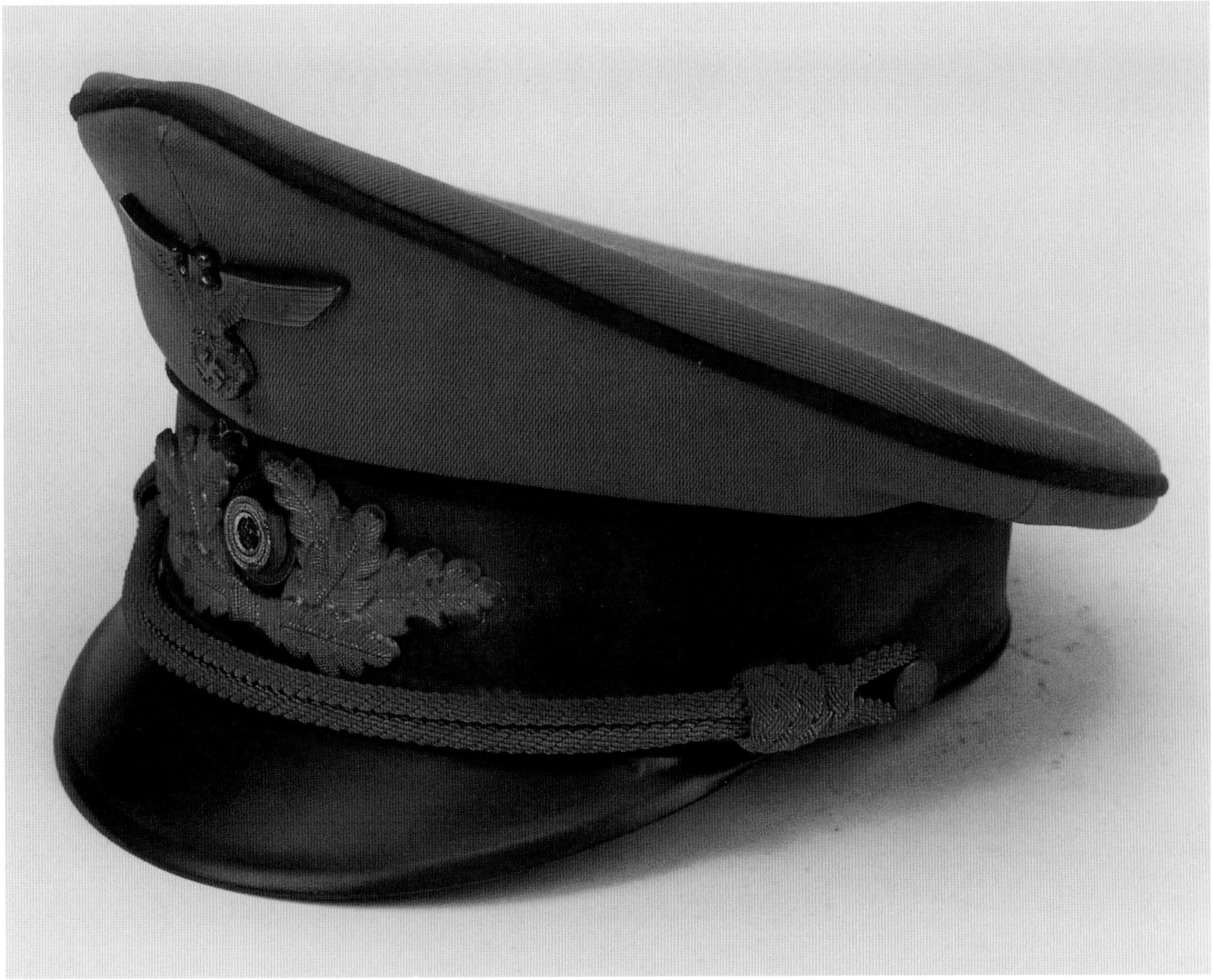

NSDAP Political Leader's "Office Dress" Tunic

This coat was worn with dark brown trousers. Rank was indicated by collar tabs and insignia of function level was shown on the sleeve title. The color of the sleeve band piping indicated the state group "Ortsgruppe." This example was made in Italy. Also shown is the matching visor cap.

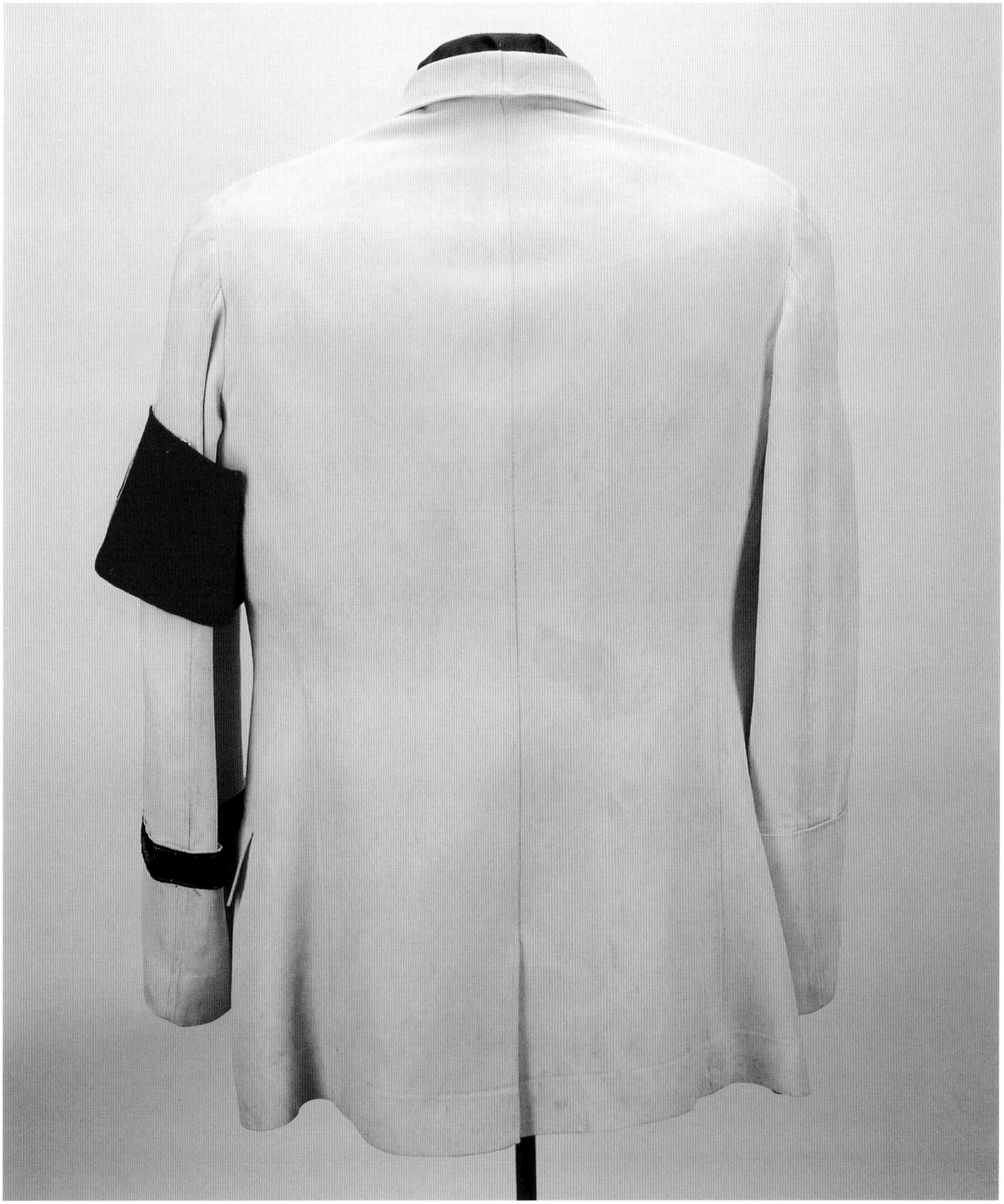

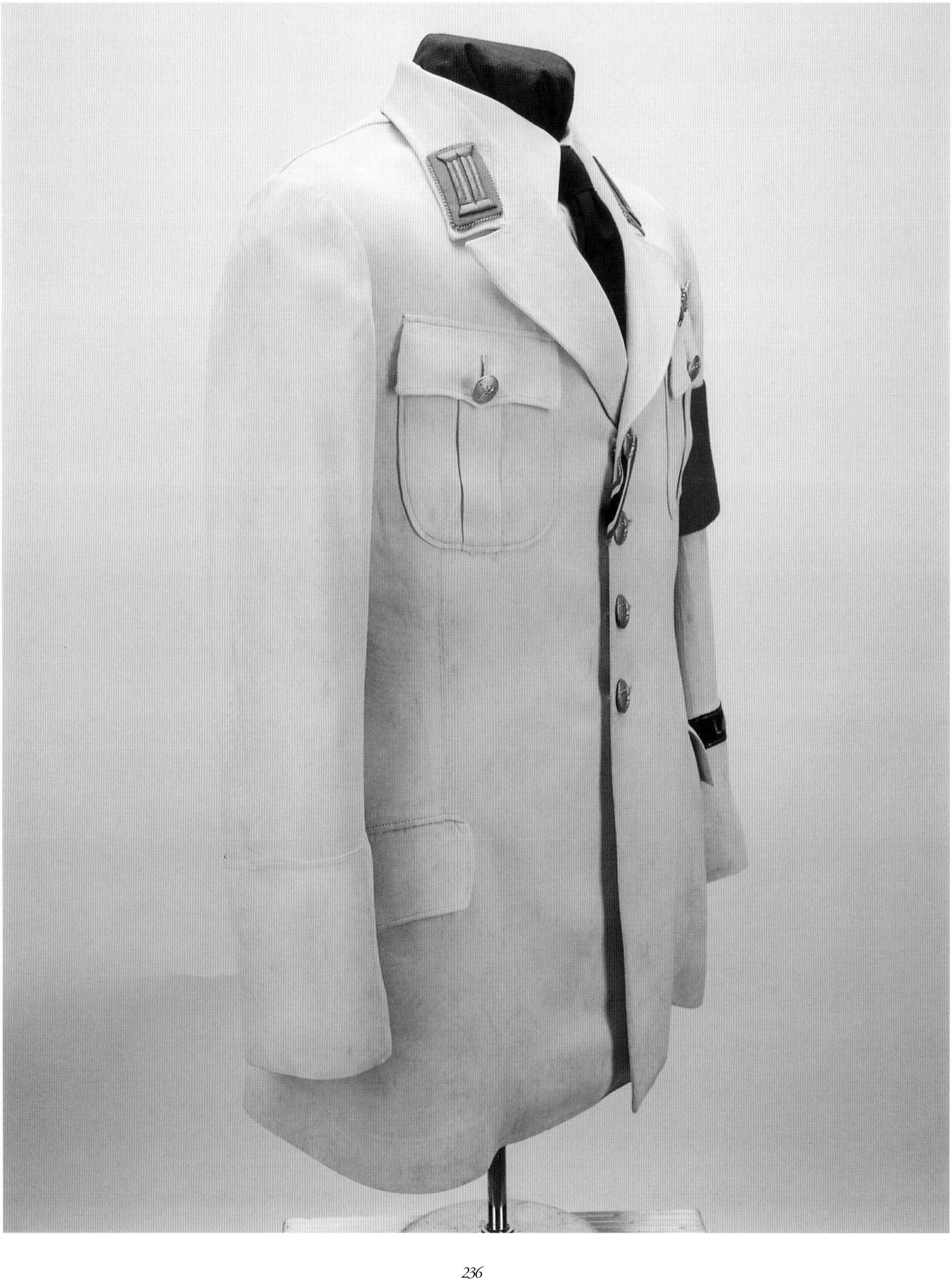

Landesgruppe in

BERRETTIFICIO
PIEDIMONTE
1927
ENCOMIATO da S.A.R. il PRINCIPE di PIEMONTE
-ROMA-
via del tritone 62 e
via del nazareno 3

Hitler Youth Third Pattern Service Leader's Tunic

Olive brown wool tunic which features a "Nord Hamburg" Gebiet triangle with traditions bar on the left sleeve and an HJ arm band. The shoulderboards are black, piped in silver for the rank of Bannführer.

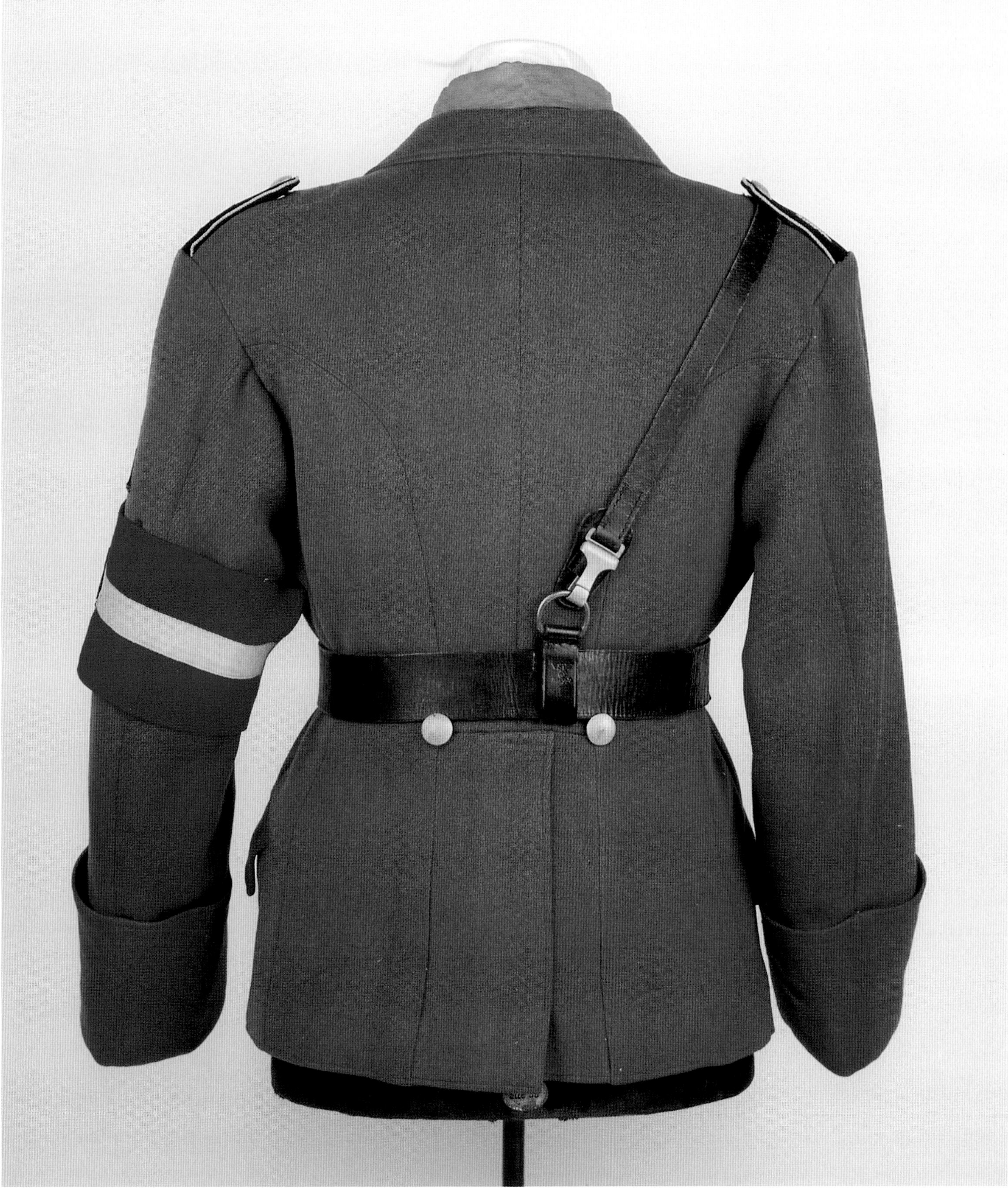

Nord
Hamburg

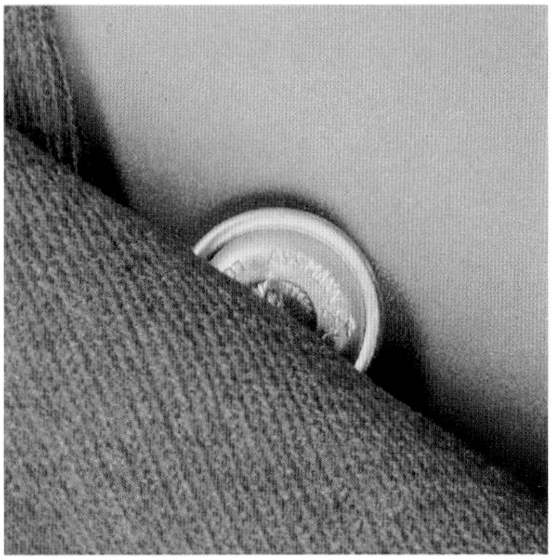

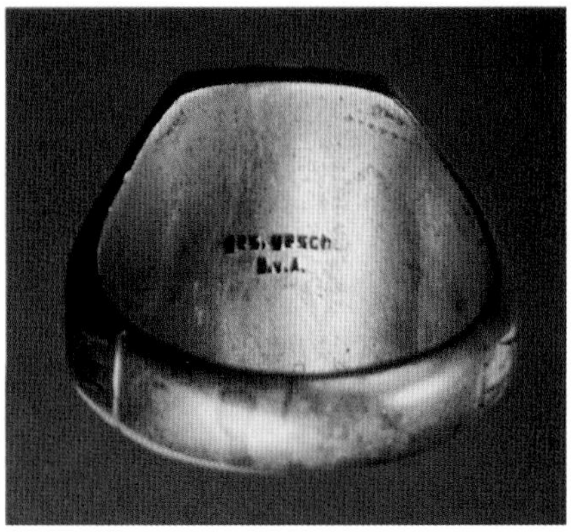

Hitler Youth Leader's ring.

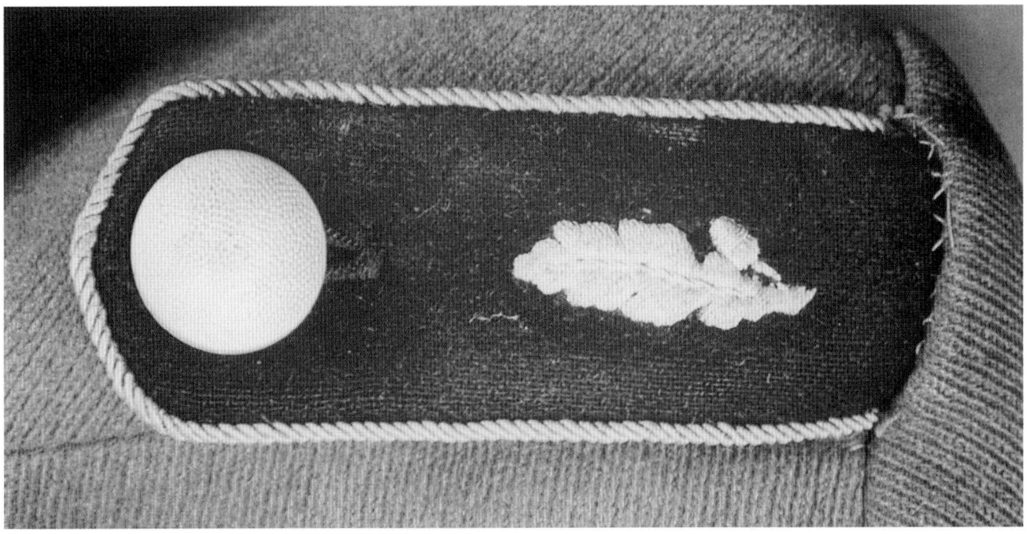

A second example of the Bannführer shoulder board.

Golden HJ Badge of Honor.

Golden Leader's Sports Badge.

Shoulder board detail of a Hitler Youth Oberstammführer.

Hitler Youth leader's visor cap.

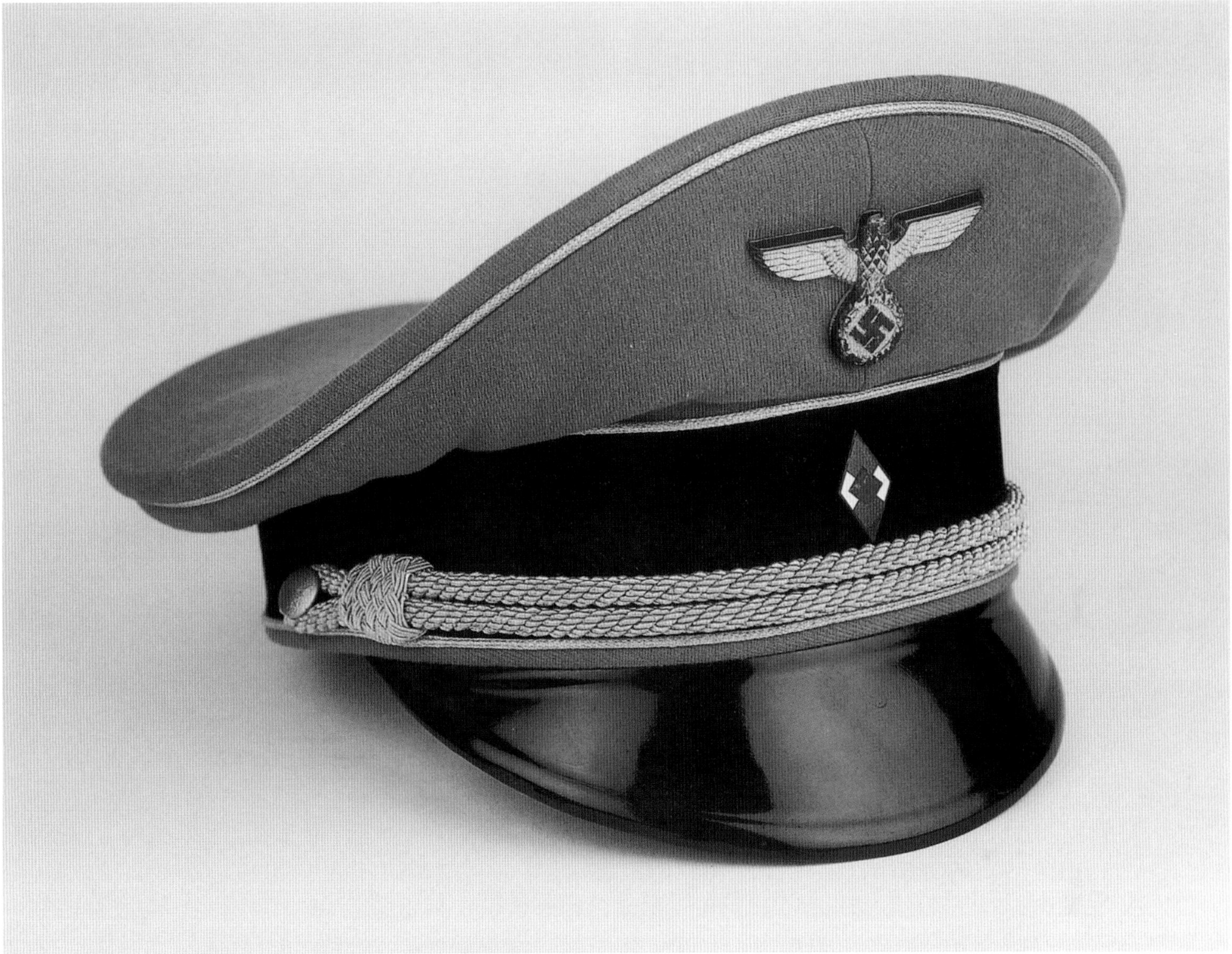

The Hitler Youth Leader's Dagger and Hangers.

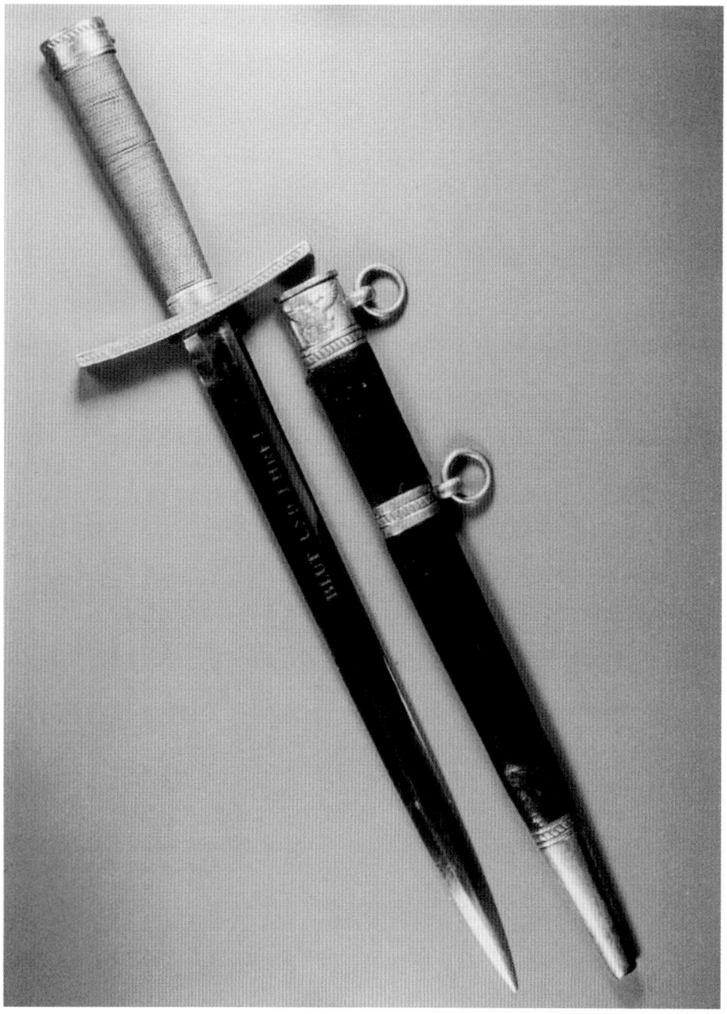

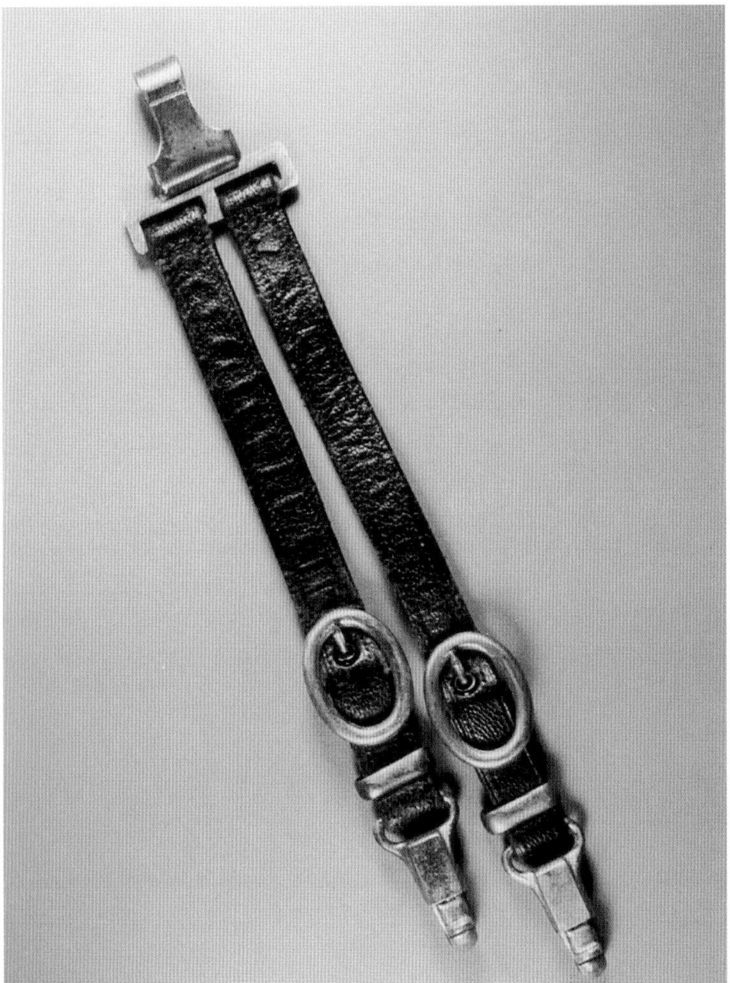

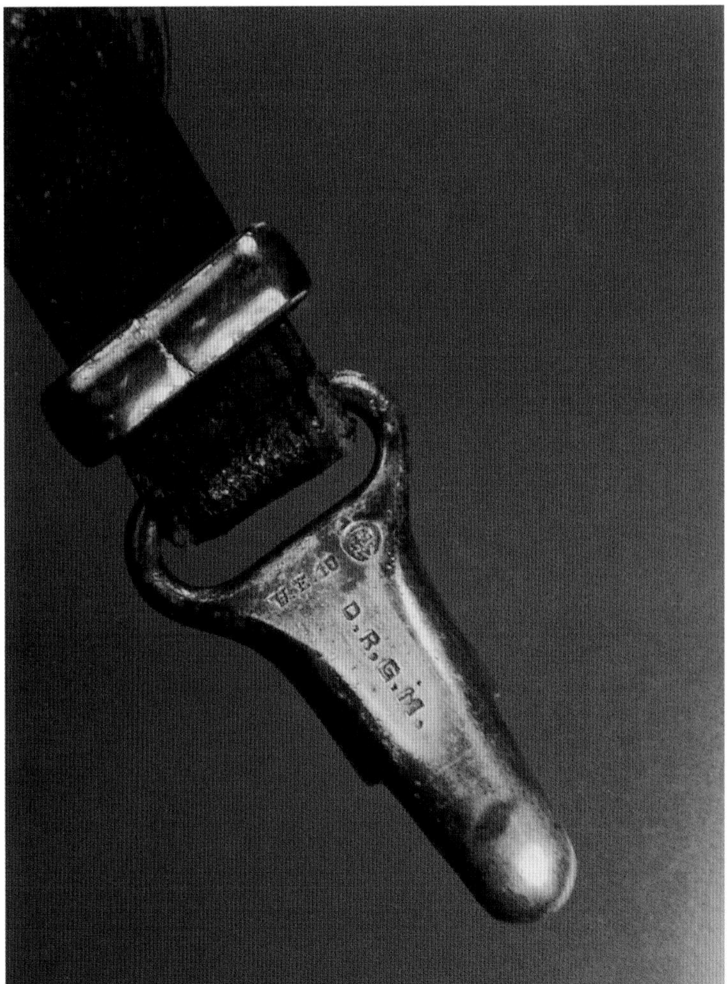
D.R.G.M.

HJ Führer Bluse

This jacket is made of navy blue wool and has metal belt ramps and leather buttons. The "Sud Hochland" Gebiet triangle, and HJ armband are on the left sleeve. The shoulder boards indicate the rank of Oberstammführer.

Size 35

Süd

Süd
Hochland

DJ
HJ

DJ Leader's cap.

HJ Membership pin.

First design HJ cap badge.

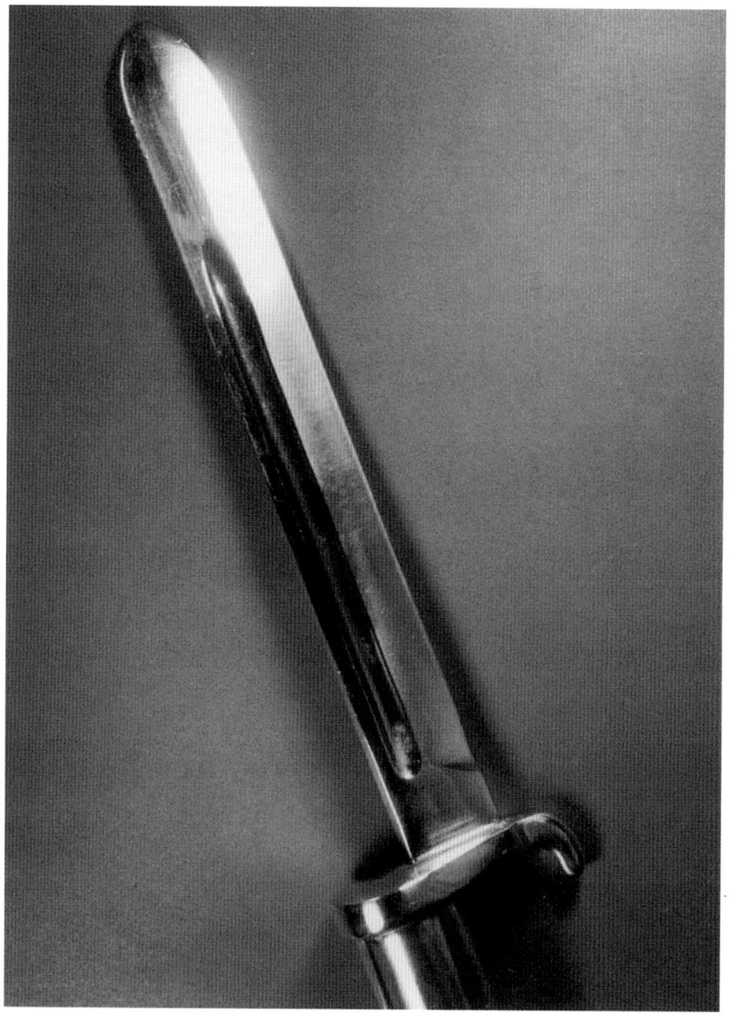

"Bayonet" style flag pole top for HJ Gefolgschaft or DJ Fahnlein standard.

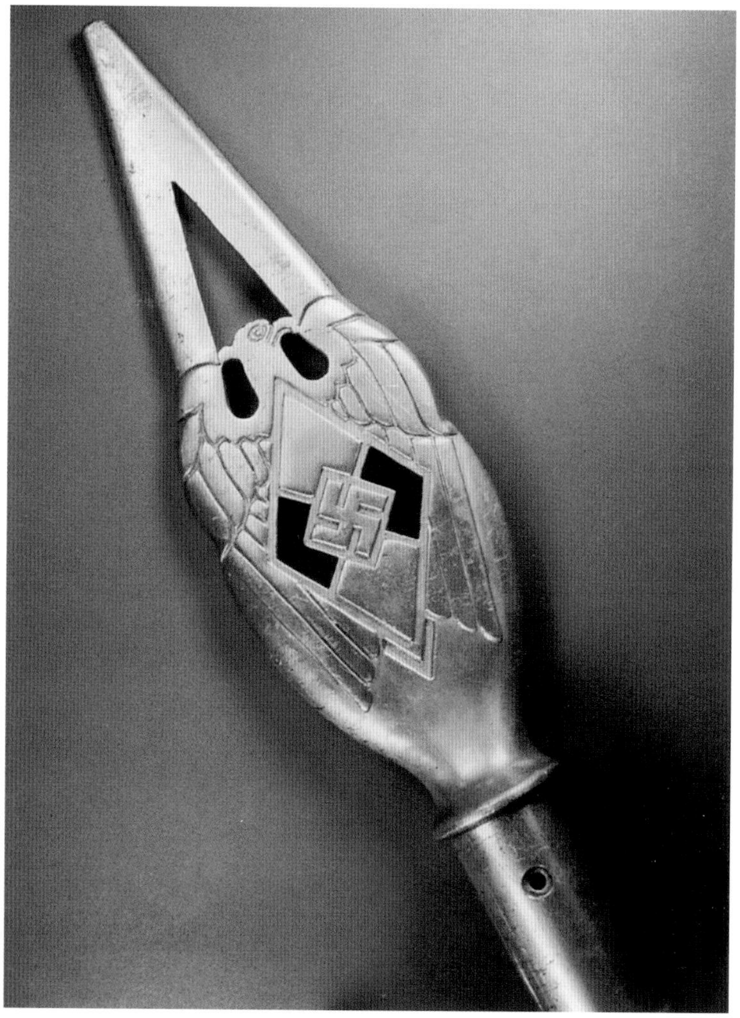

Flag pole top for a DJ Jungbann flag.

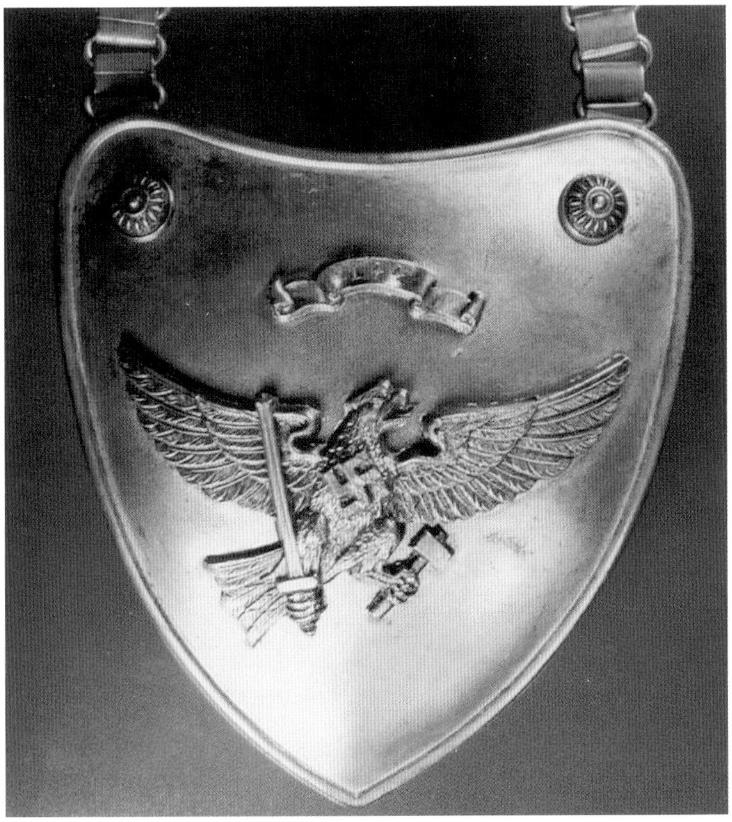

DJ Gorget for standard bearer of a Bann, introduced in July of 1938. Right: Maker's mark on gorget.

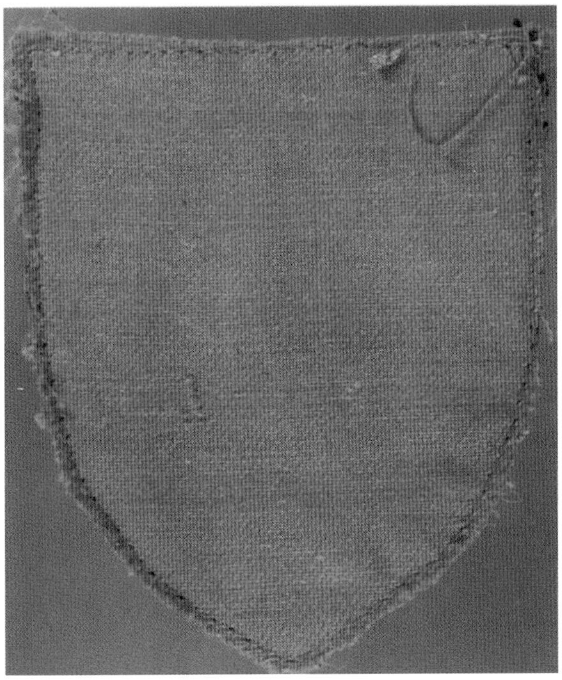

HJ standard bearer's sleeve patch.

Youth Sports Badge of the DRL.

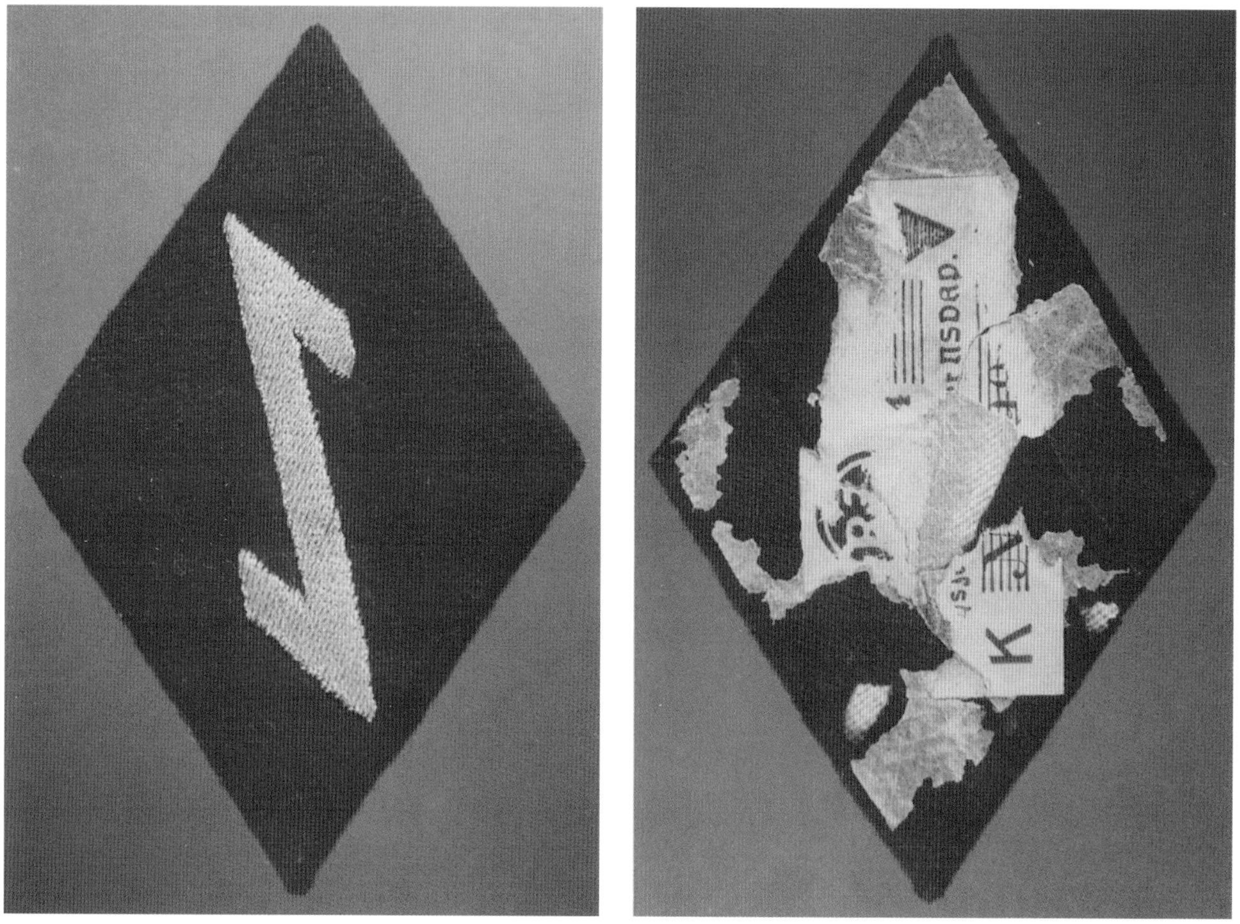

HJ adjutant's sleeve badge.

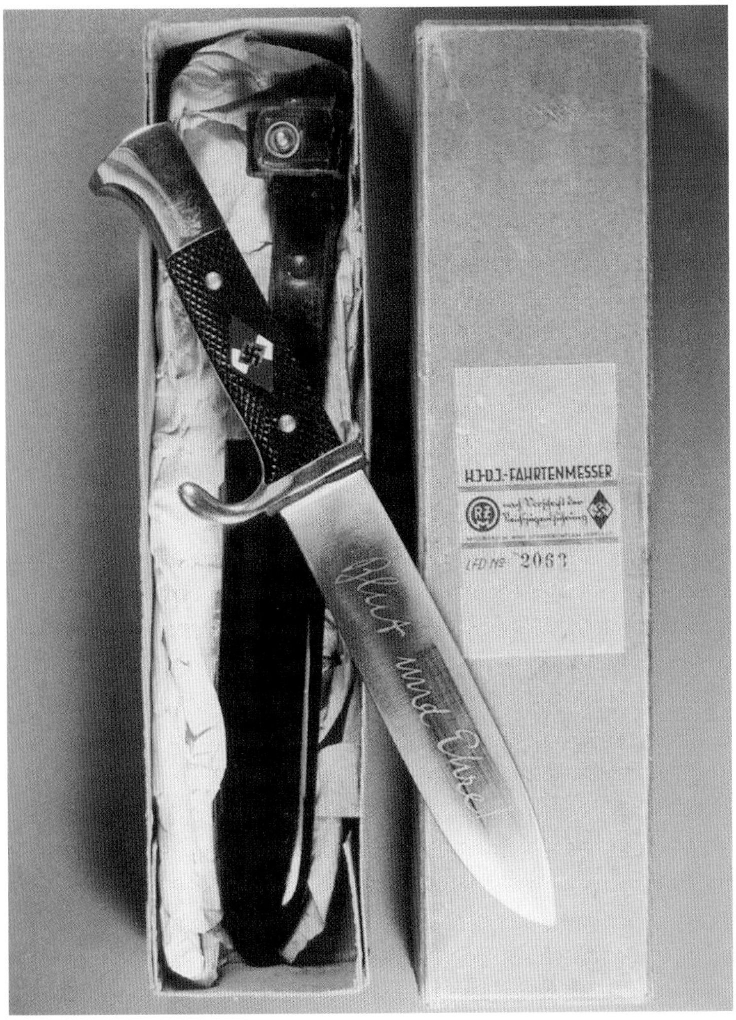

HJ-DJ knife with issue box.

Elastolin toy soldiers of the Hitler Youth.

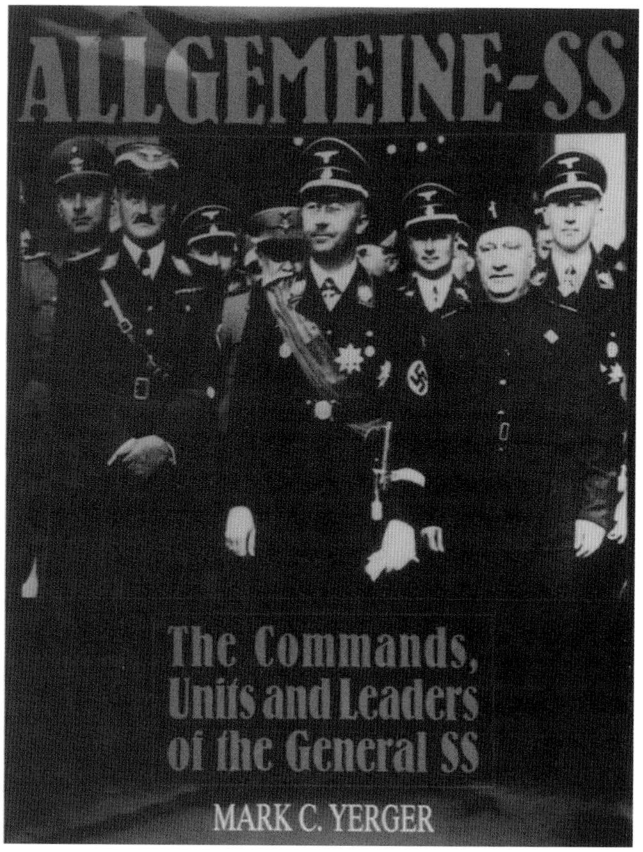

SS UNIFORMS, INSIGNIA & ACCOUTREMENTS
A Study in Photographs
Compiled by A. Hayes

This new work explores in detailed color the complex subject of Allgemeine and Waffen-SS uniforms, insignia, and accoutrements. Hundreds of authentic items are extensively photographed in close-up to enable the reader to examine and study. These items were amassed over a number of years from many noted collections. Included are: uniforms, cloth and metal insignia, headgear, field equipment, firearms, edged weapons, documents, regalia, children's toys, and an overview of medals and decorations. This book provides a rare opportunity to view a broad array of period pieces in detail. The black and white photographs are from private albums and have never been published.
Size: 8 1/2" x 11" over 800 color and b/w photographs
248 pages, hard cover
ISBN: 978-0-7643-0046-2 $79.99

ALLGEMEINE-SS
The Commands, Units and Leaders of the General SS
Mark C. Yerger

The commands, units and leaders of the General SS are finally compiled into a single detailed reference book for both the historian and SS memorabilia collector. This complete volume begins with an explanation of the twelve administrative and command main offices involving the SS to include the development, components and functions of each as well as their respective office chiefs. The following section explores the most powerful posts in the SS, the Higher SS and Police Leaders, along with the subordinate SS and Police Leaders found in occupied territories – both the commands and the individual holders of these posts are examined in depth. The SS Main Districts are covered next including all their various subordinate components, title changes, development, commanders and chiefs of staff. The more than forty SS Districts follow, detailed in a similar format. Examining the more than one-hundred and twenty-five SS Foot Regiments in the General SS, the names and ranks of the hundreds of commanders, as well as details of unit location changes, popular and honor titles as well as other data for each are within a separate chapter. Finally, the elite SS Riding Districts and Regiments are covered similarly. Career biographies are included for more than two hundred senior SS commanders, many of whom served portions of their career in the Waffen-SS, Polizei, SD and other facets of Himmler's commands. The biographical data for individuals alone adds vast detail to this fascinating topic. Along with more than 120 rare photos of SS senior ranking officers and seven maps, a detailed index allows referencing of individual commands or personalities. Mark Yerger is also the author of *Riding East, The SS Cavalry Brigade in Poland and Russia 1939-1942*; *Images of the Waffen-SS, A Photo Chronicle of Germany's Elite Troops*; and a biography of *SS-Sturmbannführer Ernst August Krag* (all three titles are available from Schiffer Publishing Ltd.).
Size: 8 1/2" x 11", over 120 b/w photographs, maps, fully indexed.
256 pages, hard cover
ISBN: 0-7643-0145-4 $49.95